UNDER TABLE MOUNTAIN

A BIOGRAPHICAL NOVEL

by
NIGEL PATTEN

Strategic Book Group

Strategic Book Group
P.O. Box 333
Durham CT 06422
www.StrategicBookClub.com

Design: Dedicated Business Solutions, Inc. (www.netdbs.com)

ISBN 978-1-60976-965-9

The last decade of the 19th century were troubled years in South Africa. Tension between Britain and the two Boer republics, the Transvaal and the Orange Free State, increased until war became inevitable. These turbulent ten years saw many notable figures pass through Cape Town at various times and for various reasons, figures like Robert Baden-Powell, Rudyard Kipling, Jan Smuts or Cecil Rhodes. All of them were friends, guests or visitors at 'Mon Desir', the home of Sir Henry Juta, barrister and Speaker of the Cape House. This is the story of Louise Juta, the youngest of his four daughters, from her birth until she left South Africa in 1904 to go to school in England and never return. She spent the last years of her long life in Switzerland. I would drop in most days for an hour or two to play scrabble with Lady Luia Forbes, as she then was, and listen to her reminiscing. This is the result.

Sir Henry Juta

Lady Luia Forbes

Louise Juta

For Luia in fond memory of the many hours we spent together.

CHAPTER . . .

1

"She's low today, sir" A slim manicured hand strayed from the thick graying mustache down over the bearded jaw. The seated passenger nodded his head out of the window and looked expectantly across the first class railway carriage at the only other occupant, who frowned slightly, as though he were not quite sure that he was the person being spoken to after all. He straightened a braided tassel on his smart red uniform jacket and raised his bushy eyebrows.

"I beg your pardon, sir?"

"The tablecloth, sir. She's low today." He glanced out of the window again. The resinous buds on the dark green spreading firs were opening and the shady acacia bushes in the impeccably lawned gardens abounded with cream-coloured clusters of blossoms. Beyond the stately homes, Table Mountain raised its huge horizontal head above the wisps of blue misty cloud. The almost permanent perpendicular layer of stratus cloud moved only when high-level gusts of wind swept in from the ocean and disturbed it. Then Devil's Peak emerged mysteriously from a swirling shroud, like some drowning giant heaving its heavy head above the maelstrom. Still puzzled, the army officer leaned forward.

"I assume you are referring to the mountain, sir." They both stared at the constantly shifting layers of cloud. The grave gentleman inclined his head and smiled.

"Indeed, sir." After forty years in Cape Province he had lost little of his Scottish accent. As a young man he had left his native Inverness to make his fortune and he had succeeded, not without a struggle at times. Twice he had found himself without a penny in his pocket, but his Gaelic stubbornness had

1

won in the end. He settled complacently in his plush corner seat. The steam engine puffed round the last long curve into Mowbray. The weather was oppressive. The onshore winds that often blew over the town and into False Bay had dropped and an uncustomary humidity hung above the peninsular. The bearded banker's irritation mounted as he remembered his mission. It would probably be another false alarm and not the first time the doctors had predicted that his daughter was about to deliver another child. And not the first time they had been wrong either. A good Edinburgh medical student could have done better! He snorted scornfully and then, as if noticing how closely he resembled the steam engine up ahead, transformed the snort into a low cough behind his gloved hand. His military companion smiled.

"You are from the Cape, sir?"

"All but the birth, sir. Married, raised a family and established myself in business here." He lost himself in reminiscences: Scotland! In 1830, the year of his birth in Inverness, the first steam railway in the north had just opened, Walter Scott was on his death bed somewhere in the Mediterranean and King George IV had passed on amid a wealth of social grievances.

The little train ground to a squealing halt. Beyond the neat suburban station buildings, tranquil unpaved roads, mere sandy lanes under the flowering tulip trees, wound lazily up the wooded flanks of Table Mountain. Gabled roofs peeped through ancient rough-barked holm oaks. The occasional thatched cottage nestled under spreading dark-boughed pines, thick with clusters of bright shining brown cones. The mountain dominated everything, sloping slowly to the south and the rich compact vineyards of Constancia.

A smartly-dressed station-master passed the carriage window and paused to raise his braided cap to the occupants. He strode on, flicking ostentatiously at the tails of his blue frock coat. The Scottish banker coughed again, this time on purpose.

"And you, sir, are not entirely unknown to me," he said. He withdrew an elegant silver card case from within the amble folds of his dark blue coat and flipped it open. His travelling companion barely raised his eyebrows as he accepted the proffered card: "Murdoch Morrison Tait. Managing Director. The Bank of Scotland, Addderley Street, Cape Town." He leant forward stiffly to confirm his identity and seemed displeased that visibly the name meant nothing to the officer in the facing seat. He cleared his throat and smoothed his trim beard.

"My son-in-law, Sir Henry Juta, has on several occasions spoken of your..." He searched for an appropriately inoffensive word. A smile flashed across the young officer's sunburnt face.

"Exploits?" he suggested. Most of the events that had occurred in the previous June in Mashonaland had not yet reached the general public. These romantic pioneering adventures had been tarnished by suggestions that Her Majesty's government had tricked the native king, Lobengula, into authorizing a British force of some one thousand soldiers to cross his lands. Sir John Willoughby had commanded the rearguard of the column that crossed the Macloutsie River on June 27, 1890 with the thoughtless blessing of the High Commissioner, Major-General Methuen. His flippant commentary at the time was the talk of the town among those in the more privileged positions.

"Well, gentlemen" Methuen had mused. "Your destination is a place called Siboutsi. I do not know if Siboutsi is a man or a mountain. Mr. Selous, I understand, is of the opinion that it is a man, but we will pass that by. You then proceed to Mount Hampden. Mr. Selous is of the opinion that Mount Hampden has been placed ten miles too far to the west. You had better correct that. On second thoughts, better not. You might then be placing it ten miles too far to the east. Good morning, gentlemen." After six weeks of struggling through swampy impenetrable bush, the expeditionary force had reached open grassland and built a fort, which they named Salisbury after the British Prime Minister.

Sir John Willoughby leaned back into the soft cushioned seat. It was his turn to reminisce. After the dull routine of British barracks life, the Mashonaland adventure had been a refreshing interlude. The banker studied the soldier closely, slowly turning his high black silk hat with the tips of his fingers.

"I'd not be surprised if you were on your way to Groote Schuur, sir," he hazarded. Not a very difficult guess. Only two possible destinations offered themselves to a famous soldier farther along the railway line: the Cape Prime Minister's residence at Rondebosch or the Naval Base at Simonstown. Willoughby nodded assent and cast his eyes back to the window and the pine-clad cliffs that climbed precipitously behind the peaceful tree-lined lanes. Above a final line of vegetation, Devil's Peak appeared about to tumble down among the fashionable homes of Cape Town's elite. To the south-west the level plateau of the Table itself had finally shrugged off the clinging clouds and rose majestically into the dark blue sky.

Table Bay had first been visited by Bartolomeu Dias in 1488 and later became a place of call for ships passing to India. Water and food could be obtained and mail left under marked 'post office' stones, to be picked up by ships bound for Europe. The first permanent white settlement was begun by Jan van Riebeeck. Requested to undertake the command of the initial Dutch settlement in the future South Africa, he landed three ships on 6 April 1652, fortified the site as a way-station to supply ships bound for the East Indies. Van Riebeeck was Commander of the Cape until 1662, charged with building a fort, improving the natural anchorage at Table Bay, planting fruit and vegetable gardens and obtaining livestock from the indigenous Khoi people. By the end of the seventeenth century, the town had taken shape. The gardens and the brick castle, which replaced the fort in 1666, were surrounded by streets lined with warehouses, taverns and company offices. The style of living resembled that of Holland, but the climate caused the traditional Dutch architecture to be considerably modified.

As a result of the Napoleonic Wars, the British annexed the Cape in 1806. The emancipation of slaves and the opening of the Suez Canal in 1869 had dealt a severe blow to the town's prosperity.

The little train pulled out of Rosebank. Willoughby sighed and tapped out a rhythm with his fingers on his leather brief case.

"These are troubled times, my dear Mr. Tait." He wondered if it were worth his time pursuing the conversation, but his inquisitive companion was obviously not going to leave him in peace for long. The train rumbled over the river bridge where the Liesbeek brook flowed under the line. Named after a small river in Holland, the first free burghers of the Dutch East India Company were granted land to farm along the stream in 1657. It sprang to life in mountain gorges and later joined the Black River to empty into Table Bay at Paarden Island. Willoughby grunted and tried to look irate. "General Machado's at the bottom of it, sir. No need to look beyond him. Sending in criminals like Gouveia to tamper with the natives!" The banker had heard talk about Machado at his father-in-law's table. Machado was Governor-General of Portuguese East Africa. Although a gentleman himself, he did not hesitate to employ a renegade agent called Gouveia in his service. This released criminal terrorized much of Mashonaland with his own army of undisciplined black mercenaries. "Why, sir, you must have heard how, only a few weeks ago, he had the impudence to pull down the Union Jack at Umtasa."

"My son-in-law told me, however, that Jameson had returned with encouraging reports," added Murdoch Tait, twirling his immaculately furled umbrella between his feet. Willoughby snorted.

"Jameson! He'd say he had a good trip no matter what happened! And then laugh about it." Many people had fixed ideas about the infamous Dr. Jameson who had the overall command of the Salisbury expedition. The Scottish doctor—everyone seemed Scottish in Cape Town—had created for himself an ambiguous reputation since his arrival in Kimberley thirteen years before to take up a medical practice in the booming diamond town. Born in Edinburgh in 1853 and a graduate of University College, London, Dr. Starr Jameson had abandoned a brilliant career in England and allowed a whim to take him to South Africa. At Kimberley he had become close friends with Cecil Rhodes, then a young man establishing his fortune in the diamond mines. With Rhodes' rise to political importance, Jameson became his chief confidante, undertook several missions to Lobengula, the Matabele king and was responsible for persuading the hoodwinked king to let the expedition through to Mashonaland. Jameson went on to explore the route to the east coast from Salisbury. On his return, Rhodes, now Prime Minister, had appointed him administrator of Mashonaland. With his dour Presbyterian upbringing, Tait disapproved of Jameson's ungentlemanly methods. What for some might pass for bravery, to him such behavior was simply irresponsible.

"Why sir, I hear that Jameson lost all his clothes, except for one dancing shoe and all his stores but for a 7lb tin of icing sugar! He broke three ribs. He burnt down an entire native village by accident. He allowed himself to be capsized by hippopotami, plagued by marauding lions and then, if you please, finds the whole thing a fine joke when the natives laugh at his undignified appearance!" Carried away by his wounded sense of propriety, he looked up sharply when Willoughby made a noise that sounded suspiciously like the beginnings of a chuckle. The banker frowned. They were all the same, these expatriate soldiers who had chosen to exile themselves from civilized England to explore the African bush.

Brakes screeched, heads appeared at windows and the train pulled into Rondebosch station in a cloud of steam. An unusual number of people of all ethnic groups milled about on the platform or simply sat around on the benches. Rhodes' residence at Groote Schuur was a few minutes' walk away and most people preferred the train journey out of town to the dusty carriage ride. Willoughby stood up and straightened his jacket. Almost before the train had ground to a halt, the door opened and the station master, cap in hand, stood ready to receive the distinguished soldier in person. A compact crowd of colored servants hovered outside the white railings, hoping to catch a glimpse of some well-known political figure. In an assortment of brightly-colored head scarves and skirts, they clashed quaintly with the flowering tulip trees in the avenue and contrasted vividly with the pale purple mountain slopes beyond.

Among them a young man waited patiently for the mob to disperse. Dressed in white flannel trousers, shirt and wide-brimmed hat with a colored band round the crown, he recognized Willoughby and pushed through the crowd with outstretched hand.

"I was afraid I'd missed you, sir. We had a bit of trouble up at the house and I was delayed in leaving." The Prime Minister's private secretary, Harry Currey was an efficient intelligent young man with a gift for organization and a reputation for caustic comments. It was not clear which of these two qualities had attracted Rhodes and resulted in his present privileged position. Uncharitable gossip suggested other darker motives for the nomination. A native South African born on the veldt, unsophisticated and frank, Rhodes' capriciousness and fickle character had initially confused Currey. Even more so Rhodes' obsession with secrecy.

"Mr. Rhodes does not want any living man to know him," Currey would explain to admiring friends. "His whole life and interests are mapped out into little squares. Any person involved in square six must know nothing of what's going on in square seven" He led his guest to the waiting carriage. "Mr. Rhodes asks you to excuse him for not coming to meet you in person. Work, you know." He fidgeted with a wide dotted cravat that had come loose around his neck.

Willoughby acknowledged the apology with a slight smile.
He hardly expected the great Cecil Rhodes to disturb his routine for a relatively low-ranking army officer. That would be
like the mountain going to Mahomet. The two men heaved
themselves into the waiting carriage, the colored servant
closed the door and the horse moved away under the yellow-
blossomed acacia trees into Belmont Road, over the railway
bridge and then climbed up the avenue to Groote Schuur,
hidden behind a curving copse of stately pines.

Murdoch Tait sat on alone in the first class carriage. The
Newlands Cricket Ground, where a match was in progress, flashed past. In their impeccably white clothes, from
a distance the players resembled bleached bugs scurrying
over a green baize billiard table. The unflattering comparison vexed the banker. As a young man in Inverness, he
had played a lot of cricket in the fields along the river with
Glen More rising from the highland mists on one side and
the salt flats of the Moray Firth on the other. When he was
not playing cricket he had liked to scramble over the rock-
scattered slopes and screes of Craig Phadrick to the ruins
of the castle where King Duncan was supposedly murdered
by Macbeth. His vigorous reliable character took its roots
there in the highlands and he was proud of the fact that
even after so many years in Cape Town their influence had
never waned.

His children, two sons and three daughters, had other
roots and traditions. All had been born in South Africa and
two of the girls had married Afrikaners of Dutch origin. In
spite of the sporadic financial crises that swept through the
Tait household from time to time, the girls had made conse-
quential marriages; Helen's husband, Sir Henry Juta, was the
foremost barrister in Cape Town and Speaker of the Cape
House of Assembly. Clara had married the owner of the larg-
est vineyard on the Peninsular. As a rule Murdoch Tait disapproved of partiality or favoritism, but he had to admit that
it was with Helen that he felt most at ease. Born in 1874, a
year marked by fierce fighting in the Orange Free State, it

was Helen who accompanied her father on his annual trips to Carlsbad for the cure. Propped comfortably on the carriage cushions with the metronomic clicking of the wheels on the rails below him, he smiled to himself. What a picture they made together! Strolling down Kaiserstrasse, a part of that dazzling wealth of aristocratic elegance. How many eyes turned to cast discreetly envious glances at the slim black-haired girl on his arm in her stylish Paris dresses, always in the best of taste and of the latest fashion! Helen's entire education and upbringing had prepared her for an eminent position in Cape Town society. She would be at ease both at genteel dinner tables among other bare-shouldered ladies in vaporous clouds of tulle and crinoline, and in her father's box at the opera. This season Nellie Melba sang sentimental love songs with the handsome idolized Polish tenor, Jean de Reszke and from the Royal Box Lady Warwick dazzled the auditorium with her very décolleté velvet dresses, a scarlet aigrette pinned in her abundance of long auburn hair. Daisy Greville, wife of Lord Brooke, the 5th Earl of Warwick, had become involved in affairs with several powerful men, most notably King Edward VII. It was not uncommon for married women of a certain social class to enjoy romances with a man higher on the social ladder than her husband, often with the husband's knowledge. The contact could also assist him in his social or political ambitions. Lady Warwick's main flaw was that she lacked the ability to keep her love affairs private. For her indiscretions she had earned the nickname 'The Babbling Brooke' and was the inspiration for the popular music hall song 'Daisy, Daisy'.

Murdoch Tait's day-dreaming came to a sudden halt as the train squealed into Kenilworth station. He saw the stationmaster at the far end of the acacia-shaded platform with its well-tended flowerbeds a blaze of multicolored heart-shaped pansies. He was arguing with well-contained dignity with an old lady who was trying to take possession of a suitcase in the luggage van. Seeing the banker climb down from his carriage, the stationmaster abandoned the old lady and scuttled down the length of the platform. He had been accidentally struck by a passing cabriolet some years previously, which had damaged one hip, so that he advanced diagonally like a crab and attracted much admiration.

"I'm afraid they haven't sent the carriage, Mr. Tait," he panted, closing the carriage door behind the banker.

"Very well, Watkins, I'll walk."

"Thank you, Mr. Tait." He touched the peak of his cap and scuttled back to the old lady, who had finally managed to persuade a colored porter to load the suitcase on a barrow.

Murdoch Tait left the platform and turned into Kenilworth Road, like all the other thoroughfares along the railway line, little more than a sandy lane bordered by beautiful gardens and stately homes. The absence of the carriage had irritated him at first, but he was forced to admit that his son-in-law had probably driven over to Groote Schuur and his daughter's carriage had taken the children away from the house while the new baby was being delivered.

A few minutes later he strode through the pair of imposing wrought-iron gates between two brick pillars and passed into the welcome shade of the spreading silver firs. Built like a true highlander, short and stocky with an almost pugnacious gait, the banker followed the graveled drive under the trees. The spring sunlight fell as scattered beams and mottled shadow over the carpet of dry pine needles accumulated round the cracked scaly bark at the base of the trunks. The Juta house stood at the far end, backing onto the mountain, surrounded by meticulously mown lawns and borders of flowering shrubs. The April weather had woken the white stars of lepelhout and where the trees thinned and enough sunlight penetrated, clumps of yellow lobelia fringed the lawns.

As he approached the house, colored gardeners stopped their work in the borders to raise their caps. From behind the imposing house came the sound of greenhouse frames being moved. Less than ten years old, Mon Desir had been designed by Sir Herbert Baker along traditional Dutch colonial lines. Gray slate gables rose against the towering backdrop of Devil's Peak and the deeply eroded ravines that scarred the sparsely-covered upper slopes. Here the Liesbeek bubbled from the heart of the mountain before flowing gently between sandy banks to Bishop's Court and into the residential suburbs of Newlands and Claremont. From the wide-open window of the day nursery a white linen curtain fluttered and flapped against the oiled teak shutters. Brilliantly-colored bracts of purple and orange bougainvillea climbed in disorderly abundance over the pale stucco walls. Murdoch Tait glanced at the flapping curtain as he crossed the croquet lawn. It seemed too much like a flag of truce. A dreadful doubt entered his mind. What would the new baby be? A boy at last, or yet another girl—the fourth!

The Sikh butler, looking very smart in a freshly-laundered white coat, black trousers and green apron, with a startling orange turban hiding his long braid of hair, arrived at the massive front door in time to take the banker's hat, coat and umbrella. Murdoch Tait raised a bushy eyebrow in guise of a question. The butler walked ahead to the foot of the wide teak staircase, an impressive sweep of polished wood, blue carpeting and bright brass rods leading to the first floor landing.

"I am thinking Mr. Tait, sir, that if you was to go upstairs now..." A fractional smile of pure unaffected joy, so spontaneously apparent among the Cape colored and Indian population, disturbed the mask of deferential respect, the traditional hallmark of all domestic staff. The normally imperturbable banker only just hid his surprise and disapproval at this display of sentiment on the part of a servant and climbed the staircase, his leather boots making no noise on the thick blue carpet. For once he failed to pause in front of the display of miniature palms in the jardinière on the landing. They reminded him of Helen. Her passion for gardening, especially exotic hothouse plants, occupied much of her time. Murdoch Tate stood aside to allow a uniformed nurse to slip past and hurry down the stairs with a white enamel basin. Without time for the usual curtsey, she vanished round the bottom of the banisters like a scared rabbit. So that was how he still affected people! With age creeping up on him, his reputation for blunt Scottish intolerance no longer gave him any satisfaction. The years had softened him. He marched down the long teak-paneled corridor to his son-in-law's dressing-room. He found Henry Juta sitting on the window seat in conversation with Nanny. He got to his feet, smoothing down his trousers at the knees.

"There you are, sir. I was wondering if my message had reached you at the bank."

"Not for nothing again I hope, Juta. Not for nothing." His fingers caressed the silver side whiskers, remarkably bushy for his seventy-five years. Henry Juta smiled. Tall and well-proportioned, he possessed a northern charm and elegance typical of certain aristocrats from the flat wind-swept plains and polders of Dutch Friesland. Born in The Hague in 1859, the barrister had only been thirty years in Cape Province. Already with a solid reputation back in Holland, his father came from a family known to have settled there over six hundred years earlier. He had suffered a serious throat complaint in his son's second year and lost his voice. His career at the bar collapsed. On the wise advice of a specialist the barrister had taken his family to Cape Town, famous for its temperate climate. He founded a company importing law books written in Dutch and later his own printing house, Juta & Company in Carlyle Street. Of his three children only Henry had remained in South Africa, steering a delicate political course between allegiance to his adoptive country on one hand and fidelity to his Dutch origins on the other. Both daughters had married and left Africa, Willa going to Scotland and Louise into the central prairies of Canada. The future of the Juta name rested squarely in the capable hands of Henry. Part of his success at the Cape Town bar and later as Speaker of the Cape House derived from a sense of tranquility and dignified counterpoise that reassured and created confidence in his colleagues. By now he knew how to tackle his uncompromising

Scottish father-in-law. He spread his hands wide and smiled reassuringly.

"No indeed, sir. It's all over. Shall we go down to the study? I haven't been home long myself. Mr. Rhodes is screaming about our Portuguese neighbors again." He could still hear the Prime Minister's high falsetto voice: 'They're a bad race, Juta. They've had three hundred years on the coast and all they've achieved is to be a curse to any place they've occupied!' At the foot of the staircase Murdoch Tait turned sharply.

"Come on, Juta. Stop hedging. Tell me the verdict, man! What's my daughter produced this time?" At the end of the spacious marble-floored hall a maid pretended to be engrossed in her task of polishing the brass door handles but with one discreet ear on the conversation. Henry quickened his pace, the familiar look of philosophical compromise on his imperturbable face.

"Well, you are aware, sir, that we were more or less certain a month ago. The doctors all predicted it. The names, you know, we'd decided upon before Christmas: Louise, after my mother and Aunt Louise, of course, and..." The banker stopped dead in his tracks, his white whiskers bristling.

"My God, Juta! Can't my daughter produce anything but girls?" His powerful voice rang throughout the vast house. It silenced the chatter downstairs in the kitchen. Even the gardeners weeding the flower borders under the windows unbent their aching backs and suppressed grins. A door on the landing clicked shut. In Helen Juta's bedroom the nurses were dutifully washing and dressing the baby with none of the male chauvinistic prejudices so audibly demonstrated by the irate banker. He snorted like bull confronted with a red cloth. A fourth daughter in a family where pride was paramount! In upper class society women were treated as princesses in public, but at heart their husbands and fathers and brothers adhered to the traditional conviction that women were an inferior sex, weak, capricious, frivolous and ineffectual. They fully exemplified the French maxim: 'Sois belle et tais-toi!'

A woman was a lovely possession to be paraded in public on condition that she never opened her mouth.

Henry sighed. He too would have preferred a boy at last but, being irreproachably devoted to his wife, would defend her to the bitter end, even against his formidable father-in-law.

"Perhaps we should go into the study, sir," he suggested, "and we can.." He was about to say 'celebrate' but rapidly changed his mind and the sentence remained unfinished. The discerning banker had understood perfectly and snorted again, but as he too disliked the idea of servants overhearing heated family discussions of any sort, he allowed himself to be guided into the secluded study. In large houses with an army of servants rumors spread like lightning through the neighborhood grapevine and invariably figured as topics of conversation at the next day's afternoon tea within a radius of at least five miles. Murdoch Tait, however, stood his ground and prepared to return to town, muttering into his beard something about not having time to waste on ... the word 'girls' was left understood. He had already taken his hat, coat and umbrella from the butler when an upstairs door opened and they heard a confused gurgling noise followed by an explosive cough, which soon developed into an ear-splitting wail. The banker glanced over his shoulder.

"Well, Juta, at least she can make herself heard!" He marched out of the front door and in less than ten seconds had vanished down the curving tree-lined drive.

Two miles away Sir John Willoughby leaned back on the upholstered leather of the lurching carriage and closed his eyes. The drowsy drawl of Rhode's secretary on the seat beside him had begun to irk him. Yet in some ways the young man's conversation was refreshing for its total lack of hypocrisy. The political and diplomatic world tended to be ruled by the principle that you never said what you thought, even to your closest friends and family; especially to your closest friends and family! Harry Currey said what he thought, which both disturbed and mystified the more conventional colonials in Cape Town society, who had never lived in the bush or faced anything more dangerous than a runaway horse. Harry Currey's clear blue eyes looked you straight in the face, daring you to speak your mind. It was this natural ingenuousness and spontaneous naivety that had attracted the Prime Minster, as being in direct contrast to his own obsessive introversion. Together they made a well-balanced working team.

They drove past a massive Victorian mansion set in rolling grassland dotted with ancient oak trees. The gently undulating land rose to a low wooded ridge. A herd of deer grazed peacefully in the sun-dappled shade. Willoughby waved his hand at the bucolic scene.

"What house is that?"

"That's Westbrooke House, sir. It used to belong to Mr. Tait, the banker." The secretary replied.

"Used to?" He remembered his recent travelling companion, so stiff and starched, and couldn't imagine the dour Scot living in such an exquisitively romantic setting. Harry Currey grinned and his blue eyes twinkled.

"Well yes, sir. Mr. Tait has the well-known habit of losing fortunes as fast as he makes them. To such an extent that one can't help wondering if he does it on purpose." Having never had a fortune to lose, Willoughby lost interest in the matter, and they sat in silence until the line of white columns, stepped eaves and black slate roofs of Groote Schuur, literally 'Great Barn', appeared partially masked by the dark green foliage of numerous broad-leafed firs. The sandy drive dipped into a hollow, densely carpeted with ornamental eriobotrya shrubs. The sweet-scented white flowers had mostly finished and been replaced by scores of golden-yellow fruits the size of a plum. Several imposing stone pines grew closer to the house and shaded it with their umbrella-shaped crowns. The English architect, Sir Herbert Baker, had been commissioned by Rhodes to convert and refurbish the traditional Dutch colonial house, after a fire had recently badly damaged the building. Little of the original house remained. The traditional thatched roof had been replaced by sturdy

Welsh slates. Most of the lovely old wooden furniture from indigenous trees and impossible to replace had burnt. Baker rebuilt the front of the house, added a long stoep in the back and constructed a new wing, containing a billiard room and master bedroom on the second floor with a large bay window overlooking Devil's Peak. The resulting blend of classical and Dutch South African styles had succeeded beyond the architect's dreams.

Rhodes had made the gardens his personal sanctuary. Recuperated from the arid slopes of Devil's Peak, once covered in native karroo shrubs, Rhodes insisted they should be 'masses of color'. Surrounding the house was a wealth of roses, hydrangeas, arum and canna lilies, bougainvilleas and fuchsias. He encouraged visitors to walk there, so that they might share with him the beauty and the thoughts the gardens inspired. Rhodes told his guests that he liked to think people would continue to roam down his paths long after he had gone. Farther away from the house on the slopes of Devil's Peak, Rhodes kept antelopes, zebra, eland, wildebeest and ostriches.

The carriage swung round a curve in the drive. With the mountain now behind them, the two passengers gazed down over the coastal flats, progressively submerged by the tentacular city suburbs, stretching from the silver line of the sea to the foot of the mountain. The dominant position of Groote Schuur had become an appropriate symbol for the famous man who now lived there. Several guests had gathered on the stoep. In deep wicker chairs they chatted or simply contemplated the purple mist-wreathed cliffs beyond the hydrangea beds. Rhodes sprawled indolently in an old armchair with one foot propped on the rungs of a dining-room chair. Dressed in his habitual white flannels and tweed jacket, he fidgeted with the omnipresent felt hat perched on one knee. He was holding an animated conversation with a pale asthmatic lady in an outrageously elaborate straw hat. Willoughby tried to recall what he knew of the notorious statesman.

Born into a family of eleven at the vicarage of Bishop's Storton in 1853, Rhodes grew up a grubby little boy with fair ruffled hair and a precarious health, later diagnosed as tuberculosis. At seventeen he joined his older brother in Natal where they attempted to grow cotton but abandoned the farm three years later and moved to the Kimberley diamond mines. The next eight years spent mostly at Oxford University installed in him the conviction that the Anglo-Saxon race was at the highest point of evolution and that his aim must be to secure its predominance through British expansion, particularly in Africa. Even during the Oxford years Rhodes had been building his fortune at the diamond mines, founding a firm contracted to pump out flooded mines. He began purchasing claims and by 1880 had become the biggest claim holder in the De Beers Mining Company. A year later he entered politics as member for Barkly West, a rural constituency comprised mostly of Dutch farmers. From 1882 Rhodes became more and more obsessed with the idea of expansion northwards. He dreamt of a railway from the Cape to Cairo, running through territories occupied exclusively by British settlers. With his colossal fortune he founded a Chartered Company and obtained government sanction to push the frontiers of British-held territory farther north. He tricked Lobengula, the Matabele chief, into giving his company concessions north of the Macloutsie River. In May 1890 the Prime Minister, Sir Gordon Sprigg, was defeated over a railway construction bill and resigned. Rhodes stepped in.

As he climbed down from the carriage Willoughby studied the man on the verandah, already a legend in his own lifetime; a tall broad-shouldered man with unruly auburn hair, carelessly brushed over his forehead, eyes of bluish gray, dreamy but kind, deep lines on his face following the curve of his mustache. His mouth possessed a determined, masterful and somewhat scornful expression. His face and corpulence showed signs of flabbiness and physical neglect.

Whatever aptitude he may once have had for sports, seemed to have abandoned him.

"I do believe you're a misogynist, Mr. Rhodes!" The pale lady waved her fan at him. It was common knowledge that the Prime Minister insisted on having male secretaries. Rhodes burst out laughing in his alarming falsetto voice.

"Not at all! I don't hate women. On the contrary I like them. I simply don't want them fussing about me." Again he laughed, but nervously this time. Perhaps he was conscience of the fact that absence of a family life handicapped him in some way. A wife and children might have softened the asperity and frank brutality visible in his dealings with humanity. A wife could have kept an eye on his precarious health. She would have protected him from the malice of disappointed female admirers like Olive Schreiner sitting opposite him, trying to reanimate the sentiments she had felt for him before her departure for England.

Olive Schreiner was a name known in both South Africa and England for three reasons: she was the elder sister of William Schreiner, the Attorney-General. Together with his colleague and friend of university days, Henry Juta, he was considered among the foremost lawyers in the land. Olive was author of a best-selling book: 'The Story of an African Farm', written during a period when she was governess to various farming families on the veldt. The weeks in isolation, surrounded only by the rolling grasslands and the colored farm workers, had formed her imagination and heightened her sensibility towards any form of injustice, a sentiment aroused by the racial and national conflicts on the increase in South Africa at the turn of the century. She had always wanted to be a doctor, but had never had enough money to pay for the training. She decided she would be a nurse, as that did not require payment, but ill health prevented her from completing any form of training and she suffered the first of the asthma attacks that plagued her for the rest of her life. During her time in England, the renowned sexologist, Havelock Ellis, wrote to her about her novel, and their relationship soon developed. Ellis would later scandalize much of society with his work on human sexual behavior. At select evenings he entertained his guests by performing tricks with his penis. Olive had formed a deep and long-lasting affection for the unorthodox physician, passionately devoted to Olive before she returned to South Africa. Ellis had in some sort replaced the hero-worship she felt for Rhodes in the early days, shortly after the publication of her book. She communicated this feeling to her brother in a letter.

"Rhodes is even higher and nobler than I ever expected. Our friends, however, are so different that we could never become close. He spoke to me more lovingly of 'An African Farm' than anyone has ever done." After her return from England, though still believing in his greatness, she had opposed his native policy and eventually numbered among his severest critics and political enemies. As usual she wore an embroidered Bavarian dress that made her look even more robust than she was. A massive woman with a face that could have passed for male or female, her many posts as governess and her transient lifestyle had left her little time for romance, although she had once become engaged under doubtful circumstances. It had not lasted long. She developed a deep interest in freethinking, philosophy and the critical importance of woman's equality.

On the stoep Rhodes had tired of the conversation. He turned his moods on and off like a tap. At his elbow a servant quietly replaced the ice bucket and produced another bottle of white Cape wine. The wicker chair creaked as Rhodes leaned forward to pour himself a second glass. A horse whinnied in the stables at the rear of the house. A narrow-winged lammergeyer soared into sight over Devil's Peak. Even at that distance the contrast between its creamy front and dark tail appeared noticeable. Rhodes followed the slow wheeling flight.

"Look at that bird up there," he said. "Doesn't it make you feel as though you're walking between earth and sky? And when I look about me," he waved his hand at the towering mist-shrouded mountain and then the silver ribbon of ocean behind the clustered streets of the city below, "I say that such a paradise shall be English. I look up every day and say that the English shall rule this earth." All heads turned in his direction. Because he had in fact been talking to himself, he seemed surprised and turned red. Like most introverts he made a very poor public speaker and was painfully conscience of the fact. He noticed the latest arrival and waved his hand.

"Willoughby! Good of you to come at short notice. I shan't have to detain you long." He introduced Olive Schreiner who listened dutifully to the officer's stereotyped compliments on her famous book, which he had never read. Rhodes beckoned to his secretary in conversation with a bent old man who had once been someone important somewhere.

"Set out those new maps of Gazaland in the study, will you, Harry. You know, the revisions of the Pungwe estuary that Jameson brought back." Harry Currey darted through the blowing curtains at the open French windows and Rhodes turned back to his visitor, toying distractedly with his bushy blond mustache."What's new in the enemy camp, Willoughby?" he inquired, a badly-suppressed trace of mockery in his high-pitched voice. It was common knowledge that the Prime Minister had little time for soldiers. He considered the average military man as having very little brain and a vast amount of incompetency, and deeply regretted having to call on the army from time to time. He preferred sending eccentrics like Jameson with a handful of picked adventurers, rather than entrusting a mission to a whole battalion of regular soldiers. Unfortunately once again the Portuguese were threatening to rupture the Anglo-Portuguese convention of 1890 that allowed the British a right of passage to Mashonaland through the port of Beira. They had established a blockade at the mouth of the Pungwe River and bullied the local chief, Gungunyana, into breaking the treaty he had made with Jameson the year before. Willoughby had been commissioned to sail north with a regular army detachment and sort things out.

"But isn't that most frightfully dangerous?" exclaimed the lady with the fan, rolling her pale globular eyes at the elegant officer in his trim red uniform. Oliver Schreiner had real reasons to fear their Portuguese neighbors. Her father, a German Lutheran missionary, had often recounted stirring stories of Portuguese cruelty and atrocities. Rhodes glared at the apprehensive lady.

"Not a bit! Not a bit!" he shouted, waving his hands irritably. "They'll only hit him in the leg! Only hit him in the leg!" He heaved himself out of the chair and strode along the verandah with Willoughby close on his heels.

Olive Schreiner glanced at her watch. She had promised her brother, Henry Juta's closest friend, she would drop in at 'Mon Desir' for news of the baby.

The two South African barristers had studied together at Oxford. Of Anglo-Saxon origin, William Schreiner being German and Sir Henry Dutch with a German mother, the sister of Karl Marx, they had both held official posts in Cape Town. Inevitably they had formed a close and lasting friendship. Olive called for her carriage to be brought round.

As she rumbled through Claremont she recognized Murdoch Tait hurrying in the opposite direction towards the station and muttering to himself. Olive smiled cynically. She need not bother visiting the Jutas after all. The banker's face answered her question. She tried to remember what names had been earmarked should the baby turn out to be another girl. She couldn't remember any of them.

2

The year 1895 dawned to a climate of uneasy political change in South Africa. Cecil Rhodes had been obliged to form an alliance with Jan Hofmeyr, the leader of the Afrikander Bond, an organization of Dutch farmers. They constituted a majority of the Cape electorate. Together they aimed at healing many of the Anglo-Afrikaner tensions in the colony. Southern Bechuanaland was incorporated as a new province, but in the north, the Transvaal president, Paul Kruger was becoming more and more difficult. He had tried to damage Cape trade with the Transvaal by increasing the transport rates over the Transvaal railway sector to prohibitive levels and by closing the Vaal drifts to prevent the alternative transport of goods by wagon.

In England the Conservatives under Lord Salisbury won the elections and Joseph Chamberlain mobilized considerable working.-class as well as middle-class support for a policy of crusading imperialism, choosing himself to take over the Colonial Office.

Such distant political mutations barely rippled the serene surface of 'Mon Desir', except that Henry Juta seemed busier since his friend Schreiner had become Attorney General. The uncertain future of the Rhodes-Hofmeyr partnership monopolized much of the conversation at dinner tables. The number of visitors to 'Mon Desir' increased.

An early May mist was rising from the damp lower slopes of Constantia, the vast sweeping hump of terraced vineyards that occupied the land between the sea flats and Hout's Bay. It had rained in the night. The Juta children listened to the heavy drops splashing on the timbered eaves outside the nursery window. Gusts of wind off the bay lashed the pine boughs at the far end of the immense lawn. Sporadic streaks of lightning scarred the scree-fanned flanks of Devil's Peak rising into its blanket of clinging cloud. They illuminated the southern sky beyond the lace curtains, creating a ghostly dance of light and shadow on the polished wax surface of the round nursery table with its miscellaneous muddle of coloring books and paint boxes. Finally the rising sun chased the storm out to sea, where the scattered cloud banks ceased to be little more than illusionary islands on the pale Atlantic horizon. From the freshly-washed slopes of Table Mountain, soft and humid, rose the immemorial redolence of damp earth and newly-mown grass.

Outside in the garden little Louise squatted at the edge of a flower bed. With grunts of intense concentration she tried to dig in the damp earth with a mud-covered trowel. An equal quantity of mud clung to her hands, face and sailor suit, a fact that seemed to escape her notice, or to be of little consequence, as the four-year-old continued methodically turning over the soil. From time to time she peeped up at the mountain, mouth slightly open, eyes wide, the muddy trowel clasped in her chubby hands like a religious relic. She seemed to be wondering what lay behind that beautiful towering miracle. How did one capture it, inhale it like the cigar smoke her father created? She recited her prayers every night. She thanked God for loving her, but He had never told her how He had created Table Mountain. The nursery and flower beds were very simple, trivial and private things, like sitting on Nanny's knee. The seemingly ubiquitous mountain was altogether different.

A clod of mud flew onto her lap. She brushed it off impatiently. Bijou, a white fox terrier puppy and a present for her fourth birthday, was in the throes of a systematic excavation a few feet away. The digging dog had approached dangerously a clump of forget-me-nots, a very sacred clump being nursed to maturity as a paternal offering. Louise's life had barely begun, but with a precocity stimulated by the atmosphere of culture and creativity at 'Mon Desir'. Yet her miniature world still centered round two overwhelming priorities: just 'being' and trying hard to please her father. Almost a mission, it suggested a bond between them that didn't manifest itself so strongly between Henry Juta and his three eldest daughters. In her baby mind existed also the idea that in some way she had to atone for being just another girl, when she knew how much both her parents had wanted a boy. People remarked that this close tie was reminiscent of the bond between her own mother and Murdoch Tait. Maybe bonding—or bondage—was hereditary. Louise alone of the Juta girls never tired of the trips to the coast, where her father loved to fish, or their exciting rambles up the mountain in search of orchids. The other sisters, particularly Renée, preferred the less strenuous sport of drawing-room repartee or musical evenings, although playing an instrument for an hour or two in front of a host of admiring guests could also prove most exhausting for small girls under twelve years old. Sometimes they had to exhibit their knowledge of history and geography, imparted with angelic patience by Miss Palmer, the governess. In the bright sunny schoolroom they also studied French and German with Fraulein Winzer, who came out from town three mornings a week.

At four Louise felt no attraction for all that stuff. From time to time curiosity or boredom might incite her to peep into the schoolroom. She might even be persuaded to sit stoically in the corner with a box of colored crayons and listen with half an ear to Miss Palmer reading aloud from Arthur's 'History of England.' But the only place where Louise felt really happy was outside observing, registering, and remembering: the colors at sunset, the wind-tossed sea off the Cape, where the Indian and Atlantic oceans clashed, the nautilus shells gathered on the beach, the swaying pine boughs, through which the magic mountain peeped at full moon, the collared turtle doves in pairs on the gabled eaves uttering their curious three syllable cooing. The standard reply to her questions about origins—that it was all God's work—left

Louise a little confused. To her, God was essentially long meaningless prayers and fearful threats of retribution in the mouth of Lady Abercrombe, during one of her Sunday afternoon 'goodie talks'

A second clod of mud, aimed better than the first, caught Louise under the chin. Crumbs of glutinous clay oozed down her neck and under the collar of her sailor suit. She grabbed the white ball of struggling fur in her fat little arms.

"You naughty, naughty Bijoux," she scolded, brushing a layer of caked earth off the dog's nose. "Don't you see those flowers? They're for Papie. What will he think if they're all broken?" She heaved a deep sigh. A weighty decision had to be made and weighty decisions at four years old over-exerted the mind as much as the imagination. "I'll have to punish you. You shall sit in the corner tonight. Do you hear? In the corner!" Bijoux, however showed little signs of contrition. He manifested more interest in chewing the hem of Louise's dark blue skirt. A needle-sharp tooth caught in the lining, which produced a bewildering series of gargling growls from inside the skirt. The puppy's subsequent contortions almost knocked the girl onto her back.

A door at the side of the house banged and voices drifted across the croquet lawn. Her three sisters were out looking for her, which meant that the time for morning gym exercises approached. Well, let them come and find her! Silly exercises! Jumping up and down and waving your arms about! There had to be more important things in life than that. She remained sat on the damp earth with the wriggling puppy in her lap. Another decision to be made! She had learnt to doubt the wisdom of provoking elder sisters. They had the disturbing habit of taking revenge by submitting her to what they called 'bravery training'. This entailed chasing her round the garden with a furry orange caterpillar. There had to be pleasanter ways of learning how to be brave.

"Lou! Linger! Where are you?" Their pet name for Louise was Linger Longer Lou, because of her habit of dawdling and arriving late for everything. The voices continued from the far end of the lawn. Her sisters had gone to see if she had hidden in the tree house. Louise licked her dry lips and wrestled with her dilemma.

"Where is the child? We'll all be late again." That was Renée, the slim dark-haired twelve-year-old. Her heavy-lidded brown eyes gave her an almost oriental look, very far from her blond Dutch ancestry. She already showed signs of the artistic sensitivity that would eventually draw her into the world of painting and writing in France for most of a life that ended tragically with her suicide during the Second World War.

"You know what Daddy said would happen if we were late again." Helen, named after her mother, was chubby like Louise with a mass of black curly hair. She played the violin and talked of one day going to Berlin to study.

"Oh, gosh!" Brenda's irate voice emerged from the rain-soaked shrubbery where she had trodden on a sheltering frog. Louise giggled and kissed Bijou between the eyes. Only two years older than herself, Brenda's bright blue eyes, fair hair and turned-up nose gave her an air of Anglo-Saxon aristocracy. Visibly she descended straight from the Tait side of the family. Louise and Helen were obviously Jutas. And Renée? No one could guess where she came from.

The sound of heavy boots crunching the gravel on the drive set the girls in a flap. Sergeant Perkins had arrived. He walked over from the Wynberg Barracks every morning, when it didn't rain, to give the Juta girls their gymnastics. Their father insisted on this daily ritual, as he did their cricket coaching from an England professional who had settled in the Cape for health reasons. From her crouched position in the flower border Louise heard the sergeant's broad cockney.

"Mornin' Miss 'Elen. Are we all set then? 'Allo! Where's Miss Louise? We can't start withart 'er."

"Miss Louise!" Nanny stood in the front porch, hands on hips, a no-monkey-business expression on her wrinkled face. Louise sighed again. Even Nanny, the wonderful old colored Nanny, who always found a comforting word of defense when everyone else scolded. She felt a twinge of baby resentment to think that Nanny should be abetting her sisters and Sergeant Perkins. Nevertheless, it was unusual for Nanny to be in front of the house shouting. Her father hated noise. Something special had happened. Louise peered carefully through the acacia bushes. A thin wisp of spider silk touched her forehead and she brushed it aside. Nanny stood on the front steps muttering. Her sisters still searched the wrong end of the huge garden. Sergeant Perkins waited patiently on the lawn among the parallel bars and mats. He looked very stupid. They all looked very stupid. Nanny called again but in a loud whisper this time.

"Miss Louise! Your papie's waiting. Be a good girl now." Louise wrinkled her brow thoughtfully. What new trick had Nanny found? Or was her father really waiting for her? Perhaps he intended to take her with him into town. It had happened before. And not just to the dentist's either! Another dilemma presented itself. Finally she sighed, tucked the wriggling puppy under her arm and crawled out of the bushes. Henry Juta appeared at the door before Nanny had time to utter a word. He glared at her filthy clothes and the equally dirty dog squirming in her arms. It almost embarrassed him to scold her. It was clear that she should have been a boy; always rummaging around in the bushes or trying to break her neck climbing trees. He only pretended to be angry.

"Look at you, child! This won't do at all. I asked Nanny to call you in ten minutes ago." He glanced anxiously at his watch on its gold chain and slipped it back in his fob pocket. He turned impatiently to Nanny, "The child's not fit to be seen! Take her upstairs and give her a bath at once. I want her washed and dressed down here in fifteen minutes." He strode off the porch, ignoring Nanny's reproachful glance. He disappeared round the side of the house in search of Peter, the coachman, to arrange to have his carriage brought round to the front. Like all the servants in the big houses of the Cape wealthy, Peter was not the coachman's real name. Whether they were Indian or Zulu or Hottentot, gardener, butler or coachman, they all had English names. Life at 'Mon Desir' was in all respects identical to life in the great country houses of Buckinghamshire or Kent. It was both a tradition and a measure of self-protection against a general malaise. They had colonized a land that did not, after all, belong to them by heritage.

Louise followed Nanny up the great teak staircase to the first floor bathroom. Stripped of her muddy sailor suit she stood at the window and waited for the bath to fill. At a time when, even in England, ninety percent of homes had no bath, this too was a luxury reserved only for the very rich. She could just see the gym area on the lawn over the shrubbery. Sergeant Perkin's voice drifted through the open curtains on the warm May breeze, punctuated by girlish giggles and outraged cries of alarm.

"Put yer futt hout! 'Old yer 'ead erect now! What the 'ell do yer think you're adoin', Miss Brenda?" Nanny tutted and closed the window. Rising steam from the bath clung to the pane and ran in snail-like runnels down the misted glass.

"Where are we going, Nanny?" Louise asked, busy squeezing water out of a punctured rubber duck that her German grandmother had given her for Christmas. Nanny scrubbed a bit harder.

"Why you ask me, Miss Louise? How I know what yer folks gonna do? Just you set still and let me get you all nice and proper." Louise was the fourth Juta daughter she had nursed. As was so often the case with colored servants, Nanny had become part of the family and could not imagine living anywhere other than 'Mon Desir'. She knew of cases where a nanny stayed three generations in the same family. The children spent much more time with her than they did with their own parents. If there were secrets to be kept or revealed it was to her that the girls came, never to their mother. Nanny was the omnipresent witness to all that happened in the house. She never doubted that one day she would die where she had spent all her life.

The mystery of Henry Juta's destination remained a mystery until Louise had settled beside her father on the leather seat in the comfortable horse-drawn carriage. As they trotted down the drive under the swaying pine boughs, she felt very important. Her silly sisters were still skipping over ropes or rolling about on the coconut mats under the hawk-like scrutiny of the sergeant major, who came in for a good deal of banter from his fellows at the barracks, as a result.

Louise sat as still as she could. She had heard from Nanny that well-bred ladies never fidgeted. They didn't even move as much as the marble statues of Greek goddesses you saw in museums. To keep her mind off this self-imposed immobility she contemplated the beautiful homes along Main Road, the homes of judges and statesmen and bankers. These exquisite reproductions of classical Dutch architecture hid behind high hedges of Cape box or flashed through the shining silver lance-shaped leaves of the eucalyptus groves. Out of sight, a train puffed out of Kenilworth Station towards Muizenberg. Henry Juta rearranged the white handkerchief in his breast pocket.

"Aren't you interested to know where we're going, child?" he inquired furtively, knowing full well the reasons for his daughter's lack of curiosity. In her haste to react Louise forgot that nodding was insufficient answer to a question. Her father raised his eyebrows.

"Have you no tongue?"

"Yes, Daddy. If you please, tell me where we're going." Louise smoothed her spotless sailor suit over her knees. The barrister pursed his lips. He had hesitated about bringing her along in the first place, not knowing how long affairs would keep him in town. Alarming news had reached him by messenger from William Schreiner. The two friends had decided to go to Government House to demand explanations for the rumor that Rhodes had sent a force of company militia under Dr. Jameson into the Transvaal without consulting parliament and this force had been captured by the Boers. Henry Juta stroked his clean-shaven chin.

"Well, then. As I have to go into town, I thought I might leave you at the museum." For a four-year old girl a museum might not be the most exciting place, but he knew his daughter would find enough to interest her for an hour or so. She could practice being a Greek statue if nothing else! He retired into his thoughts again. The implications of a potential conflict with the Prime Minster vexed him. A successful lawyer in South Africa relied on his ability to weather the storms of Anglo-Boer relationships. He could afford to take no sides in the deeply-rooted discord. His opinions and courtroom attitude had to remain impartial. Of Dutch ancestry, Juta had, however, married an English girl and not one of his own people. He was well-placed to appreciate the values and modus vivendi of compromise.

The carriage clattered over Westerford Bridge. The Liesbeek flowed placidly round the stone pillars. A small flock of rufous turtle doves wheeled into the air and vanished beyond a stand of thick-trunked valonia oaks. Behind the moving carriage a fine cloud of sandy dust lingered like a canopy for a few seconds before the breeze carried it away.

"Uncle Willie's coming with us," added Henry Juta and then immediately arched his eyebrows to indicate that however pleasant a piece of news this might be, well-educated little girls of her class never displayed their enthusiasm in public, and preferably not in private either. The carriage turned off the main road into a quiet driveway bordered by lofty red gum trees. They had shed their shining white bark, which littered the lane and crunched under the carriage wheels and perfumed the air with a balsam-scented redolence. They pulled up in front of the Schreiner house.

Rhodes' Attorney-General, an ardent South African, had not been born in Europe or even in the Europeanized environment of Cape Town, but in the very heart of the land at Wittesbergen, a Weslyan missionary outpost near the Basuto border. Six foot tall, broad-shouldered with a high narrow forehead, wavy brown hair, thick heavy eyebrows and blue eyes, it was William who, of the twelve children born to the German missionary, had inherited most from his father. He had spent his childhood among the natives along the bloodstained north-east frontier. Since his return from Oxford, where he had met Henry Juta, William Schreiner had decided to fight for a better relationship with the colored tribes in the north. Often absent in the veldt arbitrating claims of miscarried justice, he worked himself into one nervous breakdown after another, because he refused to allow people to badger him into abandoning a fight. His sister Olive's success as a writer and pro-Boer agitator sometimes overshadowed his own impact on society, which tended to overlook the quiet patient incessantly-industrious attorney. He sat at Rhodes' right hand and steered the ship of state, as best he could, away from troubled water.

Schreiner was waiting on the front steps and climbed into the carriage. In spite of his very humble origins, like his friend and colleague, today he was dressed impeccably in a black morning suit with silk top hat and ivory-headed cane on official business.

"Well, Buddie?" Juta asked as they reached the main road and turned towards the town. "Any news?" Schreiner spread his gloved hands in a gesture of exasperation.

"I saw the PM this morning and suggested that he keep clear of the whole business. Legally he doesn't have a leg to stand on. He refused to admit anything about issuing Jameson with orders. He just shrugged his shoulders and said 'Oh, that's all right.'" Schreiner sounded tired. His national pride wouldn't allow him to remain as impartial as Henry Juta. He had always suspected Rhodes, an Englishman born in England, a common fortune- hunter who had become a millionaire grubbing for diamonds. This was the man who now held the reins of a country that wasn't even his own homeland! Juta sighed. His friend was a constant reminder that by marriage he himself had one foot in the 'enemy' camp.

"What about Jameson?" he asked. "Any news from him?"

"What news do you want? All the lines are down beyond Mafeking." The frontier town of Mafeking had been founded only ten years earlier as headquarters of the railway network between Kimberley and the newly-occupied territories to the north. Eight hundred and seventy miles north of the Cape, its proximity to the Transvaal border made it a vital military position under the command of Sir John Willoughby.

"Does the PM intend to come into town this afternoon?" Henry Juta wondered as they approached the first suburbs. They had left the immense stately homes behind in their ornate exotic parks. The homes became smaller, modest cottages behind box hedges.

"Oh, he'll be there, all right!" muttered the attorney, fidgeting with the rim of his silk hat. "He won't miss the chance of reviewing the troops, as though nothing had happened!" He sounded openly hostile now; giving vent to a suspicion that had taken root two weeks earlier, when Jameson had mysteriously slipped away from Cape Town, destination unknown. Schreiner had got wind of a series of secret meetings in Mafeking with Major Heany, a British liaison officer posted in Johannesburg. Two cryptic telegrams had surfaced concerning the Prime Minister's attitude to the Transvaal and its possible incorporation within the Crown Colony, but as nobody other than Rhodes had seen these telegrams, the mystery remained unsolved. The most alarming news came from Captain Bower, the Imperial Secretary, a man of some influence in Cape Town and an ardent enemy of Krugerism. The previous evening he had told William Schreiner that the 'revolution' had fizzled out like damp squib, but that Rhodes was still determined to spend his immense fortune in developing the North. This enigmatic bit of information had sent Schreiner scuttling to Groote Schuur for an abortive explanation. Rhodes had waved the word 'revolution' aside and insisted on showing his Attorney General a set of Delft china he had recently received from Holland. The man was impossible to pin down!

The carriage continued in silence, each passenger occupied with his own thoughts, his own problems, and his own delicate allegiances. A Dutchman by birth, Juta's attitude towards the Boer state of Transvaal had always been delicate. He respected the Boers' desire for independence from

Britain. At times he even admired Paul Kruger the seventy year-old president for his stubborn refusal to be dominated by the British in the Cape. At the same time he was forced to admit that the Uitlanders in the Transvaal were subject to discrimination. The Uitlanders were the recently-arrived English-speaking population entering the Transvaal in search of gold and diamonds. Legally they had no rights and would get none as long as Kruger was president. "Rights!" the old statesman scoffed. "Yes, they'll get them—over my dead body!" It was this uncompromising attitude that ultimately led his people into war with Britain, annexation, and himself to an exile's death in Montreux, on the shores of Lake Geneva.

Both parties had justifiable grievances, but Juta could not accept the way that Rhodes was using the volatile situation to further his personal determination to push his Railway Company through from Mafeking to Bulawayo in Matabeleland. Using the unpredictable Jameson as an emissary was even harder to accept. 'Dr.Jim' made pleasant company, but even the Prime Minister had to admit that although the little Scottish doctor had 'a good headpiece', he could also be 'a damned fool and as stubborn as a mule.'

Finally the carriage came to a halt outside the Natural History Museum in George Street. It was one of the three places Louise liked to visit in town. The Botanical Gardens and the Castle of good Hope, the oldest building in Cape Town, completed the trio. She followed her father through the impressive oak doors and across the polished marble foyer into the curator's office. Mr. Sclater was a neighbor and family friend. He willingly took the Juta girls under his wing for an hour or so whenever Henry Juta had business appointments. Louise in particular, although she was the youngest, had the most questions to ask. But with the limited concentration span of the very young she would stop in the middle of a question to gaze at a stuffed bird in one of the glass cases. Eagles claimed most of her attention with their broad wings and imposing hooked bills. She appreciated them for their rarity as well as their force. The curator explained that the eagle population on Table Mountain had dwindled owing to past persecution, the effects of poisonous chemicals and the slow reproduction rate. Louise felt sorry for the few that remained at liberty.

Juta and Schreiner drove on down Government Avenue, past the Art Gallery and Government house to the Parliament buildings. A sizeable crowd lined the steps, surrounding the harassed door-keeper and a handful of bored policemen. Raised voices rocked the vaulted porch. Hands beat ineffectively on the closed doors. The policemen looked on and yawned. The two barristers slipped round to the south wing. They both possessed pass keys to a small private door leading to a labyrinth of unfurnished corridors. The distant murmur of irate voices echoed off the bare walls like the hum of an invisible hive. The sound rose and fell in waves, a vast breathing ocean of emotional intensity. Above it all the deep bass voice of Hofmeyr boomed the loudest.

Jan Hendrik Hofmeyr, president of the Afrikaaner Bond, Member of Parliament for Stellenbosch, known affectionately as Onze Jan, 'our Jan', had divided allegiances like Juta. He had begun to drift away from the Transvaal president. He resented Kruger's reckless disregard of Cape interests apparent in his fiscal policies. Hofmeyr feared that the Transvaal, because of its sudden leap to prosperity after the gold discoveries, might soon overshadow all other Dutch influences in South Africa. He set his face against Kruger's intrigues with Germany, but Rhodes' manifest imperialism alarmed him more than Kruger and he was pushing the Cape Governor, Sir Hercules Robinson, into issuing a proclamation disavowing Jameson's illicit action in the north.

"Mere resignation is not enough, Prime Minister," he insisted. "We must issue a manifesto repudiating Jameson, suspending him as administrator and declaring that the law will be set in motion against him!" Juta and Schreiner slipped into the conference room and saw Rhodes slumped limply in his chair at the head of the table. He looked utterly dejected for once, not at all his usual confident self, rather like a bear that has disturbed a hornet's nest. The infuriated insects were assailing him on all sides with their infernal buzzing. He shook his head.

"You see, Jameson is such an old friend. Of course, I can't do it." Rather ask him to annihilate twenty years of his life, back to the early days in Kimberley with Neville Pickering, the dearest of all his friends. Jameson had first encountered Rhodes at Pickering's sickbed.

Hofmeyr continued to prowl round Rhodes' chair like an incensed pit bull. Rhodes sighed.

"I'll resign tomorrow," he repeated for the fourth time. Hofmeyr turned on his heel and stomped off to lay siege to the Governor and persuade him to draw up the terms for the proclamation of disavowal. Rhodes caught sight of Schreiner.

"Yes, yes. It's true," he admitted hastily. "Old Jameson has upset my apple-cart."

"What do you mean? What can you mean?" flashed Schreiner. "Why didn't you say anything to me yesterday when I was here?" His heavy graying beard quivered with indignation. He saw already that the ensuing scandal would probably force him to resign as Attorney General. Rhodes threw up his hands.

"I thought I had stopped him! I sent him a message. I didn't want to say anything about it, if I had stopped him." Still at heart a child, Rhodes often puzzled important visitors with his incapacity to reason like an adult, a weakness that he hid behind a harsh exterior and an ingratiating manner. In fact Jameson's telegram announcing his intention to raid over the Transvaal border with his three hundred and fifty militia on Sunday evening had not reached Cape Town until Monday afternoon. Schreiner could only wave his hands in despair at this ridiculous bit of bungling. Rhodes looked as though he would burst into tears at any moment, not because of the humiliating position he had forced on the country, but because Jameson, a friend, had let him down. The foundations to his dream of a British Africa from the Cape to Cairo had floundered. In fact nobody in Cape Town knew yet that Jameson and his troop had already been captured and led away to a Boer concentration camp. Rhodes continued to bemoan his doomed venture.

"Poor old Jameson! Twenty years we've been friends and now he goes and ruins me. I can't hinder him. I can't go in and destroy him." Henry Juta leant over his shoulder and whispered in his ear.

"Think of the press, Prime Minister. Think of the opprobrious publicity." For a moment Rhodes emerged from his stupor of lamentation. A flushed fan of color rose to his puffy cheeks. What were they all talking about? Wasn't he Cecil Rhodes, the founder of a country that carried his name? Wasn't he the richest man in South Africa? He sprang to his feet.

"Newspapers!" he shouted, his voice squeaky with righteous indignation. "Do you think I care a continental fig what the newspapers may say? I'm strong enough to do whatever I choose, in spite of the whole pack of them!" As quickly as his temper had risen it suddenly abated and he sank slowly into his chair like deflated balloon. Perhaps he saw his friend a prisoner being jeered by a mob of bearded Boers. He imagined Whitehall in a state of alert and Chamberlain, the new English Prime Minister, busy clearing himself of any complicity in the raid. Everywhere the rats were leaving the sinking ship and its headstrong captain.

"There must be no recrimination," he muttered at last. "I'll take all the blame, but it will ruin me." It sounded more like a question than a statement. Schreiner turned to Juta.

"There's nothing more we can do here. Let's go to Poole's and think it over." They went into the lobby, threaded the maze of corridors once more and let themselves out by the small side door into the balmy afternoon air. A compact crowd still littered the steps to the congested main door.

Rhodes remained slumped in his chair. He listened distractedly to the hum of voices round him. They bounced off his thoughts like water off a duck's back. Introverts could do that; retreat into themselves, safe inside the armor-plated shell, peopled only by an imagination solid enough to cast the superficial outside world into the shade.

Behind his chair a heavy bearish man paced up and down. His fat moon-shaped face drooped like an exhausted wax taper. He fidgeted ceaselessly with his short bristly mustache. A diamond miner from the old Kimberley days, Johnny Grimmer had attracted Rhode's attention with his crude but unselfish warmth, and had become one of his closest companions. Grimmer suffered from an unfortunate propensity to strong alcohol. When overwhelmed by the effects, Rhodes would pretend that his friend had 'a touch of fever'. Grimmer's presence acted on Rhodes as a blanket of paternal protectiveness, both touching and surprising. He often spoke to his patron with a bluntness that resulted in flaming rows and always ended with an apology from Rhodes. Grimmer considered the famous statesman as a great baby, incapable of being left to his own resources. He lectured his companion on many subjects like Rhodes' disregard for his health. He cared nothing for politics and never made the slightest attempt to understand them. Big-hearted and loyal, he remained deeply attached to 'the Old Man'.

Grimmer hovered behind the chair, sensing the gravity of the situation. He watched the doubt play on Rhodes' decomposed face, where the network of blue veins appeared vividly under the thin skin. The face was flushed and unpleasantly bloated. His eyes had the puffy look of someone who never gets enough sleep. The sickly face brought to mind the reason Rhodes had been sent away from the damp rainy English climate; to escape the hereditary consumption that had plagued generations of his family. The two men retreated to Rhodes' private cabinet, the only place in the vast Parliament buildings where he could feel at home. Sinking into a deep leather armchair, he reached over for the half-empty whiskey decanter. As he fumbled with the glass stopper, it slipped from his fingers. Grimmer picked it up and poured them both a stiff drink.

"Of course," he growled, you would go and make a mess of the whole business!" Rhodes bent his head meekly with a whimper. Progressively the old look of mischievous amusement returned, as he accepted the drink.

"Now that I'm down, I shall see who my real friends are." He had turned the situation in a positive direction. Like everything else it had become a game of testing friendships. "Where's Currey?" he asked.

"Old Flippie? Fighting off the press, I imagine." Grimmer chuckled. He pictured the harassed secretary trying to defend his wicked master with a complex series of rational explanations that any competent journalist could tear apart in a flash. There was no rational excuse for having ordered Jameson on a raid over the Transvaal border. Grimmer would have sent the whole bunch of paparazzi to hell!

"If it's your engagements you're worried about, I can tell you that." He knew what a bad memory his boss had and his brusque manner returned. He enjoyed bullying Rhodes. "If it's those damn cricketers you're worried about, I'd not show up!" he exclaimed, settling the matter in his own mind. Rhodes sighed. He had offered to give a luncheon party at Groote Schuur for Lord Hawk's visiting cricket eleven. It couldn't be avoided. What he really needed was a gentle stroll on the mountain, where he could be 'alone with the Alone', as he liked to put it. He needed regularly to lose himself in contemplation on the vast expanse of the open veldt with Grimmer and a handful of colored boys or on the slopes of Devil's Peak. Above the tree line, dark red druce or clumps of pale pink pypies dotted the mountainside. Numerous springs seeped from shale banks and trickled down mossy runnels and scree-clogged chines. Here he might glimpse a rare spider orchid hanging from an invisible silk thread, nodding its flared sepals in the on-shore breeze. Mostly he liked to see the Cape Flats far below, a smoldering carpet in the city's haze, while he lifted his head to the clouds.

He rose suddenly and strode decisively to the door. Cricketers or no, he would go on the mountain. Schreiner and Juta had crept off to the club to snivel; the conventional reaction in times of crisis. But conventional people never became great. In twenty years they would both be forgotten. He reached the main door and elbowed a passage through the mob of protesters, deaf to the jeers and insults that flew about his head.

An hour and a half later, Louise and her father drove back from town through the sandy suburbs along Main Road. Henry Juta had passed a disconcerting hour at the club with Schreiner, Hofmeyr and Sir Charles Metcalfe, a railway engineer and old Oxford friend. Metcalfe accompanied Rhodes on his field trips. "Come, Metcalfe", the politician would say unexpectedly, "Let's go and have a chop on the veldt." They would set off in the covered ox wagon as gleeful as schoolboys on the rampage.

After the bothersome bustle at the Parliament, the soporific calm at the club disturbed them almost more. Their own security measures had created a false sense of invulnerability. A doorkeeper prevented reporters from entering uninvited. Leo Amery, the chief political correspondent for 'The Times' had proved particularly offensive and it had been necessary to evict him from the club by force. Powerless to prevent them, Henry Juta regretted such undemocratic steps. General opinion among the club members favored Rhodes' censure for the role he had played in Jameson's raid, in spite of rumors that London had sent telegrams supporting the Prime Minister's action. Where were they? In any case, even British governmental backing could hardly be an acceptable excuse for invading a neighboring state.

The journey home through the sprawling southern suburbs seemed endless to Louise. She guessed instinctively that an event had happened to aggravate her father, and for once it wasn't something she had done. On his return to the museum to fetch her, he had departed from his habit of taking the time to stroll with his daughter through the halls, telling her stories about the animals, birds and reptiles in their glass cases. He had vanished without a word into the curator's office and after a few whispered words, taken her by the hand out to the waiting carriage.

They had covered the greater part of the long slow pull up Main Road and had just passed Harefield Road when they overtook Tom, the Sclater's Chinese cook, padding along in the roadside sand, his heavy plaited pigtail swinging across the back. His wrinkled face smiled at the world with a deep philosophical satisfaction. He desired nothing more than the freedom to cultivate his sunflowers and plod to market every morning.

"How would you like to walk home with Tom, child?" Henry Juta asked. Louise was taken unawares. On the one hand she felt the desire to stay with her idol and on the other the tempting prospect of an hour with Tom. His two enormous wicker baskets, his neat blue tunic and that bewitching pigtail always fascinated her. She scrambled down into the dust.

They left Main Road almost at once, walked past the Newlands Cricket Ground, where seven years before the first test match again England had been played and reached the Sclater's beautiful old Dutch house. To Louise the imposing white façade with its characteristic stepped porch and dark slate roofs looked like a fabulous birthday cake covered in icing sugar. It filled the clearing among the stately oak trees, silhouetted against the deep blue sky and the bare buff cliffs of Devil's Peak behind. Louise craned her little head to stare up at the crenellated gables and tall white chimneys. The drive ran in a straight line to the door under the softly swaying oak boughs. Shafts of moving shadow shimmered on the gravel and closely-mown grass borders. Louise trotted beside the little Chinaman and watched the metronomic swing of the pigtail until it almost hypnotized her and she began to totter. At her side Tom chattered incessantly.

"Little Missey like get lobely eggs? Chickens velly good. Give plenty egg to Tom. Tom make lobely spring rolls." They walked round to the back of the house. The ancient slave quarters had been converted into comfortable accommodation, where Tom spent his free hours whittling chips of wood into strange primitive figures. He had joined the

Sclater family as houseboy in Hong Kong over thirty years before. Sometimes he liked to recall their home there in the upper suburbs of Victoria above the harbor. He could still see Kowloon, half-hidden by haze on the far side of the bay and the Tai Mo Shan foothills, a gray smoky plume that seemed to levitate along the Chinese border. When the family had moved to South Africa, Tom had gone too. He enjoyed the exclusivity of being yellow-skinned in a land of black and white. Most commerce was conducted by Indians, but few Chinamen had settled in the Cape.

Louise followed the tiny cook into the hen houses and set about searching for eggs. Whenever she found one hidden in the straw or fallen behind a roosting bar, she squealed with joy and passed it to Tom to slip into his apron pocket. Beyond the hen-house netting they could follow the antics of a pair of chattering squirrels chasing each other along a eucalyptus branch. On almost every step of the ornate façade turtle doves cooed softly or strutted along the roof ridge. A warm breeze had been blowing over the Cape peninsular for several days. It came in from the ocean across Houts Bay and the terraced vineyards of Constantiaberge. It marked the transition from the hot days of December and January to the prolonged drizzles of June that left the land dripping under a silver blanket of mist.

They found twenty-five eggs and Louise had to count them three times, just to prove to Tom that she could count that far. They halted next at Tom's flower garden on the far side of the oak grove. He always gave Louise a flower to take home, a single bloom that could not be misinterpreted as presumption or audacity on the part of a humble domestic. Tom darted among the creamy pink-petaled arum lilies that he cultivated himself, drying and sowing the seeds in spring, after removing the yellowish pulp. A symbol of purity, the elegant faintly-scented flowers constituted the principal element in all bridal bouquets. Less glamorously, they also enticed many pollinating insects, a white crab spider and a tiny frog. The succulent yellow berries attracted numerous birds, which then dispersed the seeds. Tom cooked the lush dark green leaves and served them like spinach. In the wild the versatile arum lily formed large colonies in marshy areas. The leaves contained stomata which discharged excess water and prevented saturation.

Louise watched Tom's blue cap bobbing among the lilies as he sought a suitable flower. He straightened his back and sniffed the breeze.

"Plenty lobely rain coming," he predicted. "Then Tom's lilies velly beautiful. Give one to Missey for her Ma. Plenty plitty flowers. Tom velly happy." Clutching the lovely lily to her chest, Louise allowed Tom to lead her back to the end of the drive. The grey slate roofs of 'Mon Desir' appeared fleetingly through the swaying pine branches a hundred yards farther down the road. Louise turned back to wave goodbye. Tom stood in the gateway bobbing up and down ceremoniously like a clockwork blue-tit. She said to herself as she walked, that surely, after Nanny, no one in the world was as nice as Tom.

As Louise arrived at the foot of the front steps, the flat top of Table Mountain vanished inside the table cloth, the bank of orographic cloud that formed whenever a south-easterly wind blew up the mountain slopes into moist colder condensed air. First climbed in 1503 by Antonio de Saldanha, the highly resistant sandstone plateau and steep grey crags dominated the natural coastal amphitheater of Cape Town and its suburbs. Platteklip Gorge split the cliffs of the main plateau and afforded the only easy ascent route to the summit beacon. Louise longed to be old enough to one day scramble up the gorge. None of her sisters showed any interest in such adventures. She could describe to Tom the flowers she had seen, especially the salmon-pink protea, which looked a bit like a colorful open artichoke. She might even catch a fleeting glimpse of a dassie or a rooikat or even a leopard. The last lion on the mountain, however, had been shot a hundred years before.

Louise trotted over the front lawn calling for Bijou. Two gardeners stooped silently over their weeding among the profusion of exotic flowers. The faint sound of voices drifted from the open schoolroom window, where her sisters were in the process of learning all about William the Conqueror from Miss Palmer. Louise skipped the last few yards, making the gravel squeak under her shoes. She fought the temptation to burst into the schoolroom with her precious arum lily. The thought that she might be forced to linger there and endure an hour of Miss Palmer's soporific droning, dampened her ardor.

Silence reigned in the dark teak-paneled hall, except that the polished oak parquet floor creaked as she crept to the foot of the staircase. Her mother had left on her social rounds, dropping off visiting cards everywhere as persistently as a political agitator dropped propaganda pamphlets through letter boxes. Lady Helen Juta presided over the Hospital Board of Aid and involved herself tirelessly in various philanthropic enterprises. Even Nanny seemed to have been swallowed up. Louise wandered out into the back yard. A tall Zulu lad was swabbing the dairy floor. At the far end a knot of Kaffirs shoveled earth into wheelbarrows. The whiteness of their teeth, when they grinned, always surprised and fascinated Louise. Her sisters told her that this was because Kaffirs lived on nothing but Indian corn. At the end of the nineteenth century the word 'kaffir' had no derogatory implications. It derived from the Arabic 'kafir' which means simply 'infidel' and was attributed by the first white settlers to all black Africans.

Louise returned to the hall a second time just as her father came out of his study and started to climb the staircase. He flashed her mournful smile.

"I'm going upstairs to my room, child. To be quiet." He vanished round the head of the massive carved banisters. Louise continued her search for Bijou. She found Peter, the Zulu head gardener, ankle-deep in a swampy bed of orange canna lilies. Famous all over the neighborhood for his green fingers, Peter seemed able to coax anything into blossom, whether in the borders or the greenhouse. Only the lilies of the valley, sent over from England at Helen Juta's special request, invariably died on him. Despite her husband's insistent reminder that the plant only grew in the Northern hemisphere, Helen Juta refused to give up, perhaps because one of the names attributed to the flower was 'Our Lady's tears', a biblical allusion to Eve's lamentations after she was evicted from paradise.

Louise stood watching Peter work for a while, shuffling from one foot to another, aware that if she dared join him in the bog without her rubber boots and got covered in mud the consequences might be dire. She satisfied her curiosity by trying to see if she could locate one of the tiny striped frogs that inhabited the lily beds. Bijou's absence continued to haunt her and she drifted off towards the pine grove. Peter noticed the determination on her face and came after her.

"Missey, Bijou gone long way away," he said softly. "He no come back." He scratched his curly head, searching his mind for some plausible explanation. His black benevolent face lit up. "But he very, very happy. He with Jesus." Louise frowned. She tried unconvincingly to picture the long-haired bearded Jesus arriving at the front door and taking Bijou away in his arms. How could he possibly need her Bijou? He must have millions of dogs in heaven. They probably had white angel wings and slept curled up on clouds. She stamped her foot. Something had to be done about it!

"But Peter! I don't want Jesus to have him! He's mine! Papie gave him to me." There remained only the thorny question of how to get to heaven and bring Bijou back home. She marched off into the wood deep in thought. Before long she stumbled on the tiny mound of freshly-turned earth and pine needles. At first she barely gave it a glance, until she almost tripped over it. She knelt down to investigate and began to dig with her hands. To her joy she unearthed Bijou, lying on his side, curly white fur full of earth. She removed him from the hole and brushed him clean. He didn't move, except that his little head kept falling between his paws as if it were too heavy to keep erect. Louise rushed into the house clutching the dead dog.

Nanny sat darning socks in the nursery. When she saw the dead puppy she tried to take it away but Louise resisted energetically.

"Tell Bijou to wake up, Nanny! I want to play with him." The lifeless head continued to slump out of her arms and the whole body seemed strangely stiff. Abandoning her habitual calm, Nanny almost shouted.

"Now you be a good girl, Missa Looie, and hand me that dog right now. He gone away to the kind Jesus. You should be happy for him." Louise stamped her foot again. Nothing but Jesus. She clung onto the dog. How could he be gone away and be there at the same time? But something inside told her to relinquish Bijou. The realities of life had moved her on a pace. There was no returning now. That was why her father had taken her to town this morning; to get her out of the house. The looking for eggs with Tom too had been an excuse for postponing the inevitable. She stood numbed with childish grief and watched Nanny carry the body away. With the instinctive resilience of the very young, she searched for a substitute and her thoughts reverted to an old idea, the idea of having a baby brother. Everyone wanted it. Maybe if she prayed hard every night to the same Jesus who had taken her puppy, he would send her a brother in his place.

Without really understand the significance of death, Louise acquired a deep feeling for the importance of life as a precious but transitory possession. Life as she knew it at 'Mon Desir' or looking for seashells on the beaches at Muizenberg would someday end. It existed as a passage in time like the tablecloth on Table Mountain or the autumn falling of oak leaves on the lawn that the gardeners would sweep up and burn. Every night Louise prayed and six months later Lady Juta gave birth to her fifth child, a son named Jan. He was destined to become a painter and muralist who opened his house in Taormina to D. H. Lawrence in 1921 and collaborated with him on a travel book about Sardinia. The only existing portrait of Lawrence was painted by his South African friend. Jan would become American and die in New Jersey at the age of 95.

CHAPTER . . .

3

The 'Dunvegan Castle' ploughed steadily north-east through a calm January sea. The last screaming gulls had turned back to the African coast. The oily blue water slid past the bows with a subdued hiss. The foaming crests of waves spread outwards with a monotonous similitude. A school of playful dolphins raced tirelessly just below the surface a few feet from the pounding wall of moving steel. Two days earlier the liner had passed within sight of St. Helena. Most of the passengers had crowded to the rails to watch the distant smudge of land glide past to starboard and exchange views about Napoleon and how he had died there so mysteriously. One whiskered gentleman from the Foreign Office insisted that the defeated French emperor had died from arsenic poisoning. The permanent dampness of the insular climate had caused the arsenic used in the wallpaper to vaporize and pollute the air in Napoleon's villa. The twin peaks of Mt. Actaeon broke the undulating gray horizon. Minds tried to imagine how Napoleon felt when he too had first seen those summits, little prepared, no doubt, for the next seven years of exile.

In the lounge Cecil Rhodes never budged from his armchair. He had made the journey so many times. At least once every eighteen months he sailed back to England to preside at important meetings of the Charter Company. His present mission differed. He wanted to avert the government inquiry in the Jameson Raid. Public outcry had insisted that Jameson be put on trial. After all, someone had to take the blame for a fiasco that had made Britain a laughing stock. Rhodes realized that he would have to take the brunt of the opprobrium attached to his infamous conduct in condoning and encouraging Jameson's project. Rhodes anticipated an embarrassing meeting with Joseph Chamberlain, the Colonial Secretary who had received nine days advanced warning of the raid and had done nothing except cable Rhodes to 'hurry up'. Chamberlain was as much an imperialist as Rhodes. "I believe the British race is the greatest of the governing races that the world has ever seen. It is not enough to develop great spaces of the world's surface unless you can make the best of them. It is the duty of a landlord to develop his estate." Chamberlain encouraged investment in tropical Africa, which earned him the nickname 'Joseph Africanus'. Rhodes possessed copies of cables sent between Cape Town and London proving that the Colonial Office had influenced his actions and even encouraged Jameson's invasion. Naturally he would refuse to reveal the contents in court at Jameson's trial or before the Select Committee designated to investigate the raid. Rhodes had agreed only to pay a large compensation to the Transvaal out of his company's profits.

"This won't do, dear." Rhodes' sister Edith leant over and tapped him on the shoulder. An energetic masterful and unconventional woman, she resembled Rhodes more closely than anyone else. So much so that when she came to visit him, he always handed over Groote Schuur to her and went to live in town, on the grounds that the house was not big enough to hold them both. Rhodes jumped and emerged from his uneasy doze. Beside him in the lounge Edmund Garret, the brilliant editor of the 'Cape Times', smiled encouragingly. A firm supporter of Rhodes, he treated the statesman informally, sometimes waking him up with a shower of pebbles thrown at his bedroom windows. Rhodes blinked and rubbed his chest.

"I think I shall make a thorough study of Marcus Aurelius," he declared. "Prison life is supposed to leave one a lot of free time, isn't it? A thing I've never had. Never had the time." Edith pursed her lips.

"Really now, Cecil. I won't have you talking like that. You're no more to blame for what happened than Mr.

Chamberlain. Do you think they'll send *him* to prison?" For a moment Rhodes recovered his old childish self. His mischievous eyes twinkled.

"They might," he said. "He'll probably be obliged to resign, in any case." Garret raised an objecting finger.

"They'd never accept his resignation! He's the most popular member of the cabinet." Rhodes grunted. That was true enough, as long as he refused to hand over the incriminating cables. Ambition dictated all political moves. He and the Colonial Secretary both had ambitions in the interest of the Empire. With a certain sense of shame he recollected a line from Plato's 'Republic': "There is no place in the world of politics for an honest man". Dishonesty in a just cause. Did that really count as dishonesty?

The door to the deck promenade clapped to as other passengers entered the lounge. St. Helena had sunk into the sea. They would see no more land until Lisbon. In the dining-room the orchestra was tuning up for teatime with Strauss and Lehar. The Blue Danube competed in syncopation with the clink of crockery and the hum of voices. Olive Schreiner appeared at the door on her way from the deck to the dining-room. On seeing Rhodes and his party, she crossed the room rapidly, never once glancing at her former idol. The Jameson Raid had changed everything for her. Convinced of Rhodes' treacherous complicity, she had taken upon her shoulders the burden of exposing him to the world. To do this she had written a new book in record time, 'Trooper Peter Halket of Mashonaland' which she was taking to London to be printed. In the novella she openly accused Rhodes of furthering his expansionist ambitions by the violent seizing of Mashonaland and Matabeleland, where he hoped to find gold. She guessed rightly that the imperial government of Britain sanctioned his pursuits by granting his British South Africa Company a royal charter. Olive Schreiner never lost an occasion to stir up public feeling against Rhodes, even accusing him and his private army of genocide. Her passion had driven her to accusing Rhodes of sending his agents to her cabin in an attempt to procure the damaging manuscript. People had begun raising their eyebrows at the extent of her vindictive hatred.

Rhodes watched her disappearing figure with cultivated nonchalance. Her attitude had little effect on him; an unbalanced female getting her own back for having been ignored. Only his public image preoccupied him. Mass reaction and not individual opinions concerned him. He had returned to London barely two months after the raid with his picture on the front page of every paper.

"When I arrived in London and saw the busmen and the cabbies and working men touch their hats to me in a friendly way, I knew I was all right," he boasted. "The man in the street had forgiven me." That was the only thing that counted. He dismissed people like Olive Schreiner from his mind, someone who dared to judge him and at the same time hobnob with a man like Havelock Ellis and his perverted party tricks.

"Shall we go in to tea?" Edith stood up, easing her elegant afternoon dress over her hips. Rhodes nodded.

"By all means. Where's Grimmer?"

"Really, dear. Why bother about Mr. Grimmer? He can look after himself, you know." Edith started towards the hum of conversation. Rhodes prevaricated. "I think he said he was going to sit by the pool," she added testily, taking her brother by the arm and leading him to the dining-room door. Rhodes pretended to look surprised.

"Not in it, I hope!" He turned to Edmund Garret. "Grimmer hates water. I don't believe he'd ever wash at all, if I didn't force him." He burst into his high falsetto laugh. All heads turned to follow his receding back.

They took their reserved table in the crowded room. A cluster of bow-tied string musicians on a raised platform surrounded by potted palms endeavored with only moderate success to inveigle their reluctant instruments into making melodious sounds vaguely reminiscent of a Viennese waltz. Tea cups clashed covertly. At the next table sat a very sunburnt colonel in uniform with a large walrus mustache that covered every inch of his upper lip and even part of the lower one when his mouth was closed. By contrast his eyes appeared devoid of brows and lashes, the hair bleached to invisibility by years in the tropics. Maps of all sizes and scales covered his table, together with sketches, plans and bundles of foolscap tied up with string. The untouched tea service lay dangerously near the edge of the table.

Edith Rhodes picked up the printed program for the evening's entertainment and leaned across.

"I see we're in for another treat, colonel" she whispered vampishly. Colonel Baden-Powell looked up reluctantly from his maps. He was returning to England after serving on the staff of Lieutenant-General Sir Frederick Carrington, guarding the northern borders with a force of Native Levies. Such was their belief in their commander, it was said that they would have followed him 'even to destruction, without a murmur'. So high did his name stand among the natives that they freely admitted that what General Carrington did not know about them was not worth knowing.

Baden-Powell had gained a reputation for himself by capturing and executing a witch-doctor called Uwini and then by occupying chief Wedza's stronghold. He seemed to have been born a soldier at heart. The greatest influence of his boyhood had not been his father, a priest and authority on optics and radiation, but his maternal grandfather, Admiral Henry Smyth, renowned astronomer and a direct descendant of Captain John Smith of American colonial fame. At the admiral's suggestion Baden-Powell had sat the open examination for an army commission, winning second place out of seven hundred candidates. In December 1876 he had landed at Bombay, a sub-lieutenant in the 13th Hussars. Since then Baden-Powell had served in India, West Africa and South Africa. He was taking advantage of the long journey back to England to work on the first draught of a book about his experiences during the Matabele Rebellion.

Seven months previously the Matabele people had revolted against the authority of Rhodes' British South Africa

Company. Mlimo, the Matabele spiritual leader, convinced his people that the four thousand white settlers were responsible for the drought, locust plagues and the rinderpest that had ravaged the country. His call to battle came at an opportune moment as Dr. Jameson, the Company's Administrator, had just sent most of his troops into the Transvaal on his ill-fated raid, leaving the country nearly defenseless.

Mlimo intended to take Bulawayo by surprise the night of the first full moon, after a ceremony called the Big Dance. He planned to kill all the settlers but not destroy the town, as it would later serve as the royal kraal for the reincarnated King Lobengula. Once Bulawayo had been purged, the warriors would head out into the countryside and continue the slaughter until all the white settlers had been either killed or had fled.

The rebellion, however, started prematurely when several young warriors stabbed a native policeman. Rumors of settlers being killed in the countryside spread and many alarmed families headed towards Bulawayo, where they hastily built a laager in the center of town, scattered smashed glass bottles on the ground round the upturned wagons and added barbed wire and sandbags to the defenses. Rather than wait patiently for an attack, the settlers mounted patrols under Frederick Selous, the famous big-game hunter and rode out to rescue any surviving settlers in the surrounding countryside.

Having experienced the effectiveness of the settler's Maxim guns, the Matabele never mounted a significant attack on the town, even though about ten thousand warriors had been seen in the neighborhood. Conditions inside Bulawayo, however, quickly became unbearable. A thousand women and children crowded into the city. The besieging Matabele made one critical error: they neglected to cut the telegraph lines connecting Bulawayo to Mafeking. Several relief columns formed and set out on the long trek through hostile country. Two months later Cecil Rhodes arrived from Salisbury, three hundred miles to the north, and Lord Grey from Mafeking, six hundred miles to the south. Lieutenant-General Sir

Frederick Carrington arrived to take overall command with his Chief of Staff, Colonel Baden-Powell.

With the siege broken the Matabele warriors retreated into their stronghold of the Matobo Hills. Then unexpectedly a Zulu spy brought information on the location of Mlimo's sacred cave. A scout called Burnham and the native commissioner, Bonnar Armstrong, were ordered to find the cave and capture or kill the Matabele spiritual leader. They traveled by night through the Matobo Hills and closed in on the cave. The two scouts tethered their horses in a thicket near a village of about a hundred huts filled with warriors. They advanced on their stomachs, screening their cautious progress with branches held in front of them. They hid inside the empty cave and waited until the witch-doctor entered and started his dance of immunity. They shot him below the heart and ran back to their horses with the alerted warriors in pursuit.

Such was the power of the witch-doctor that upon learning of his death, Cecil Rhodes was able to walk boldly unarmed into the Matabele stronghold and persuade the impi to lay down their arms. The rebellion had failed completely, but left four hundred settlers and some fifty thousand warriors dead or wounded.

It was during the Rebellion that Baden-Powell first met Burnham and a life-long friendship began. During a scouting patrol in the Matobo Hills, Burnham taught his new friend woodcraft, the fundamentals of scouting. Burnham had grown up in the American West during the Indian Wars and learnt scoutcraft from Indian trackers. In Africa he simply applied his art as an army scout. It soon became a vital necessity in colonial Africa and Baden-Powell conceived the idea of teaching it to young boys as well as the troops.

All these experiences he now compressed into his book. He blinked across the aisle between the tables at Edith Rhodes.

"Oh, yes. They have put me down for a musical sketch" he admitted, clearing his throat nervously. His eyes wandered back meaningfully to the maps on the table. Edith was not to be rebuffed so easily.

"Do tell us the title, Colonel," she insisted. Baden-Powell coughed again.

"Eh? Title? I don't know anything about the title yet. I haven't the remotest idea what it's going to be about even." A burst of feigned applause for the first artist of the afternoon almost drowned out his reply. A tall bony baritone had performed a comic song entitled 'I am a nervous man'. He undoubtedly was, judging by the excessive vibrato he inflicted on his audience. When his turn came, Baden-Powell rose and walked calmly to the piano.

"Ladies and gentlemen," he announced. "I see here on the program: 'Colonel Baden-Powell—musical sketch', but no title. This I regret I have not been able to supply before. To tell you the truth—er—I've only just thought of it. With the permission of the gentleman who preceded me earlier, the title of my sketch will be: 'I am a nervous man.'" After twenty minutes of songs, imitations and stories, which kept the room in a continuous roar of laughter, Baden-Powell returned to his papers, as though the whole episode had never existed.

"How do you think of things to do, Colonel?" Edith crooned admiringly. Baden-Powell smoothed his bushy mustache.

"Oh, my mind is a blank. With a single vision in it, lower half yellow, upper half blue." he replied enigmatically and buried himself in his pile of documents. Only Rhodes would have understood what he meant, with the vastness of the veldt in his own mind's eye. ; hazy yellow clumps of acacia shimmering in the heat, a boundless expanse broken only by the gleaming white sands of a river bed encased in a band of dark green reeds. Above it all stretched the immaculate blue South African sky.

The brightly-illuminated liner glided unwaveringly into the sunset, an ever-increasing expanse of white water in its wake, a blaze of unmindful humanity rocked by the oil-smooth calm of a mid-Atlantic swell, a throbbing pulse in the moist tropical night.

Seven weeks later Olive Schreiner made the return voyage under the same bewitching African sky. Her short stay in the capital had modified her attitude to Cecil Rhodes. With disarming capriciousness she now declared him to be a statesman of wonderful gifts but who had deliberately chosen the path of evil. The chill dampness of the London winter had subdued her ardor. The lukewarm reception of her anti-imperialist novella had intimidated her. The stolid support the English maintained for their South African hero, in spite of his misdeeds and incontestable treachery, had discouraged her. The fact that Rhodes had once been her hero irked her most. She refused to shrug off Jameson's Transvaal Raid. In London she had conversed with a family friend, John Merriman, the Treasurer General of the Cape. English-born like Rhodes, he had ended his relationship with the Prime Minister after the Jameson Raid and sat on the Commission charged with investigating the raid and writing the report. When lack of evidence obliged the court to acquit Rhodes, all Merriman could do was raise his arms and exclaim: "He's capable of everything!"

England in general had been a disappointment for Olive. Havelock Ellis had married a lesbian. They had spent the first night together and after that lived separate lives. He basked in the relative fame of his second published collection of essays: 'The New Spirit', a study of social reforms. Olive's first desire on returning to South Africa was to spend some weeks on the veldt. Shortly after her return she had met Samuel Cronwright, a politically-active farmer. Their shared disagreement with Rhodes over his support for the 'strop bill' brought them together. The 'strop bill' allowed black and colored servants to be flogged for relatively small offences. At first she was concerned that she would find marriage restrictive, but she had put aside these doubts and married Cronwright, who had gone north to look at some land near Pitsani. Olive agreed to accompany the Juta children on their annual holiday to the interior. This delightful idea brought back memories of her years as a governess on isolated farmsteads in the vast yellow plains.

Now she stood on the platform at Adderley Street Station. Clouds of steam rose from beneath the panting locomotive to disintegrate in whirling wisps under the iron and glass canopy of the station roof. On the opposite platform the slow train for the neighboring towns of Worcester and Townsiver inched out into the bright sunlight to a staccato last-minute slamming of doors. The excited clamor of girlish voices echoed under the glass dome. Olive picked out the Juta family heading in her direction behind an army of porters under Nanny's expert command. Olive wondered if she had made the right decision in accepting the invitation to accompany the exacting children for the weeks that their parents were away in England. It hadn't been clearly established if her role was that of governess or a friend of the family. Friendship had been put to the test by the fact that Henry Juta had finally decided to remain faithful to Rhodes, whereas her brother had resigned as Attorney-General and now openly opposed the millionaire's politics in the north. Nevertheless Schreiner, being of a less vindictive nature than his sister, had scolded her for the unnecessarily vehement belittling of Rhodes in her last book. Willie was now back in London once more giving evidence at Westminster and trying his best to 'do some little good', as he put it. Sir Henry emerged from among his excited daughters.

"Here we are, Olive. I hope you haven't been waiting too long. I'm sure it would be easier to get to the moon than have these children ready to leave on time." As always he was elegantly dressed in a tail coat and top hat. He cast a quizzical eye at Olive's eccentric Bavarian dress. The woman had never lived in Germany but insisted on wearing traditional clothing! It certainly did little to hide her unfortunate shapelessness! He repressed a movement of censure.

"Nothing should go wrong," he continued. Mr. Dumanie will have arranged for a cart to fetch you at Mooresburg. If by chance it has not arrived, you will wait for some sort of communication. Mr. Dumanie, being little used to our city efficiency, is not always a model of precision." He turned his attention to the station-master who was controlling their tickets. Olive smiled to herself. As far as she was concerned everyone in South Africa was inefficient compared to England, whether on the veldt or in the city. Everyone except brother Will, of course.

Inside the first class carriage the girls squabbled and fought over the best window seats. Luckily Henry Juta had turned his back to complete his instructions to Nanny. Olive eased her considerable bulk up the steps into the carriage. She thanked God that the barrister had not engaged her in any conversation, where their radically opposite positions might have caused bad feeling. He remained her brother's dearest friend and she curbed her notorious outspokenness for his sake. Henry Juta too was playing his part in the crisis 'trying to piece together broken china.'

One after the other the girls leaned out of the window to kiss their father. Whistles blew, the station-master waved his red flag, and the long line of brown wagons pulled out of the station. Twenty minutes later it had climbed over the Rex River Pass and begun its journey over the undulating veldt.

The ostrich farm they always stayed on during the holidays lay far out over the veldt, a tiny haven of silvery green eucalyptus trees in the vast ocean of sun-baked grassland. The mist-veiled horizon seemed to embrace the isolated oasis in a halo of throbbing heat. During the hot dry season the wind-swept plains scorched in the unrelenting sun. Skin flaked from arms and noses. Lips dried and cracked. John Dumanie often asked himself why he had left the orderly tranquility of suburban Cape Town to swelter on the veldt. Incredulous friends questioned this dubious attraction for a wilderness of dusty scrubland when, only half a day's journey to the south lay the pine-forested slopes and sheltered bays of the peninsular. A heavy inarticulate man, John only shrugged his shoulders and smiled timidly, almost afraid to confess that the isolation attracted him. He had time to probe the mysteries of his own existence. It reduced him to a brief flash of truth. It even saddened him to think of his Cape

Town acquaintances chained to their personal ambitions and craving for social recognition at all costs. He preferred to sit in the shade on his stoep at sunset and contemplate the purple outline of the Rivierberege Hills to the north or the high circling flight of crested larks.

Beyond the farthest line of fences a cloud of white dust rose into the still air. His wife left the kitchen and they stood together by the wooden rail. John Dumanie had known Henry Juta in the early days of his political career, when he had been elected MP for Ooushorn, a constituency composed essentially of farms like his own. Henry had shown interest in developing the ostrich feather trade and soon knew most of the regional farmers. He had taken a special liking for the Dumanies and each summer saw the Juta girls arriving for a few weeks on the farm.

With the outbuildings already in sight on the skyline, wire fences closed in on both sides of the rutted track, fences that trailed off into the hazy afternoon distance. Beyond the taut wire, isolated groups of dull brown ostriches pecked industriously at the sun-hardened earth, scraping the dust with their ungainly feet. Solitary male birds, conspicuous by their black back feathers, strolled sedately among the females. Sometimes the jolting wagon passed close to a mother bird sheltering as many as ten red-brown chicks under her outstretched wings.

In an age when feather boas dominated fashion trends, Dumanie and other Karoo farmers had seen the profit to be made by supplying the European market with an unlimited quantity of ostrich plumes. Politicians like Henry Juta had felt it their duty to encourage the lucrative trade. The endless enclosures isolated vast areas of open veldt, where the birds could almost believe they lived in the wild.

The lumbering white oxen drew the creaking wagon through the farmstead gates and pulled up by the wooden steps to the stoep. Dumanie lost no time issuing the customary 'marching orders'. The four sisters stood in a line before him with their hands behind their backs. In their uniform sailor suits they might have been sea cadets on the deck of a warship. Behind them in the yard, two colored boys sliced water melons for tea. Dumanie pretended to be stern.

"As you know, the ostrich enclosures are and must remain out of bounds. Not because there's any risk of you girls harming my ostriches, but because my ostriches might take an objection to your presence on their territory." This formal warning finished, he seemed to lose self-assurance and stammered. "The—er—pond is quite safe, but if a—er—snake should appear, there are always—er—plenty of boys within call. You may climb in the—er –eucalyptus trees, provided you don't—er—break the branches." At dinner, however, he had recovered enough to answer the usual volley of questions, the same as every year.

"Is it true that an ostrich can run forty miles an hour?"

"Is it true an ostrich can live seventy years?"

"Is it true that they swallow stones?"

"Is it true that if an ostrich sees a lion, it buries its head in the sand so it can't see the lion?" Dumanie raised his hand for silence.

"I heard a true story from a man who saw it happen," he began. "A male ostrich was sitting on a clutch of forty eggs when he was driven off by a pride of lions. The cubs played with the eggs as if they were balls, dribbling them all over the place. When the lions had gone, the ostrich returned and rolled the eggs back into the nest. None of them had broken and they all hatched. Now, do you know why ostriches can't fly?" Everyone shook their heads politely, although they had heard the story last year and probably the year before too. Dumanie knew this well enough but continued.

"Once upon a time, the falcon and the ostrich had a wager as to which could fly the best. The falcon said: 'In the name of God!' and flew straight up towards heaven while the ostrich, who forgot to invoke his creator's blessing, was scorched by the sun and fell to earth, never to fly again." The four girls and Dumanie's five sun-burnt children applauded. "In reality," continued the farmer "an ostrich is indifferent to heat. It can withstand temperatures of 56° without stress. It regulates its body temperature by moving its wings and panting. It stays on its feet all day, never seeks shade and only sits down at dusk."

"In the Bible it says that ostriches are bad parents," remarked Renée, always the first to show her knowledge, particularly if it might contradict somebody else's. Dumanie shook his head.

"That's quite unfair," he protested. "They are excellent parents, the female incubating the nest by day, the male by night. The biblical misunderstanding comes from the habit they have in the wild of leaving their eggs in three different places. The female buries one third under the sand in one place, exposing another third to the sun and hatching the last third in the nest. When the chicks have come out, she breaks the hidden eggs and feeds her chicks with them. When the chicks have grown stronger, she breaks the third clutch left in the sun, now covered in vermin, and this serves as food until the chicks are old enough to graze." The girls pulled a wry face at the mention of vermin.

Early next morning Louise had already disappeared up one of the tallest trees by the pond while her sisters still slept. She horrified them by the way she scrambled from branch to branch like a monkey. It was so un-ladylike! At 'Mon Desir' she had her own tree in the garden, a solitary fig tree that never gave any fruit. With Lady Juta's permission, the head gardener had constructed a platform of planks among the smooth gray branches, an exotic crow's nest from which Louise surveyed imaginary oceanic horizons.

From the top of her fig tree Louise possessed a perfect view of Table Mountain, from the first dawn blush, when the sandstone cliffs glistened in the rising sun, to the crepuscular fingers of purple shadow at dusk. The mountain held a mystical force and fascination. Sometimes her more conventional sisters wondered if she were completely normal. They had abandoned any attempt at teasing or tormenting her by questioning her exclusive right to the tree-house. They passed

below the twisted boughs and glanced up at her on her perch
in a different world to theirs. Louise could stay in her fig
tree for hours when the clement weather permitted, until
Nanny came looking for her. The half-experienced and in-
completely understood immensity of the universe intrigued
the five-year old. As the autumn evenings closed in, cast-
ing longer shadows from the base of her tree, she prayed for
the sailors at sea, whipped by the salt wind, deafened by the
breakers crashing off Kaapunt. She trembled to imaginary
visions of the murderous Atlantic swell.

The first night on the Dumanie farm Olive Schreiner settled at the desk in her bedroom to write to her brother. The
youngest of a family of ten surviving children, Olive and William had grown up close, under the eye of an older brother
and sister. Their childhood had been harsh. Although their
missionary father was loving and gentle, he was unpractical
and insolvent. The family lived in abject poverty and finally
broke up. Theo and Henrietta went north to the diamond
fields and William won a scholarship to Cambridge. He had
sailed in the same boat as the young Henry Juta.

As usual Olive fretted about her brother. He had success-
fully ridden out the storm over the Jameson Raid and just
been elected Prime Minister after Rhodes' resignation. But
in spite, or perhaps because of his deeply anti-imperialist
philosophy, the future for South African unity looked bleak.
Even if William didn't act upon her advice, she knew it comforted him to feel that he was in her thoughts, especially
when their two older brothers strongly censored his opposition to Rhodes and his expansionist ambitions in the name
of the Empire. They no longer spoke to him. Olive turned up
the flickering flame of the oil lamp and bent over the writing paper. Outside in the warm veldt night, redolent with the
sweet smell of honeysuckle, the farm dogs barked sporadically. The excited yelping of jackals beyond the perimeter of
the wire fences replied.

"Dearest Will," she wrote, "you are really the most hesi-
tant creature ever born." She sighed. William Schreiner

constantly doubted what he should do, and when he had done it, he tortured himself with the fear that he might conceivably have harmed someone by doing it. No doubt the childhood teaching of their mother, based on rigid restraint and self-discipline, had developed in the new Prime Minister a sense of strict morality far different from that of his predecessor. Rhodes' politics corresponded better to the view expressed by Lord Acton in a much publicized letter to Bishop Creighton that 'all power tends to corrupt and absolute power corrupts absolutely.' Olive continued writing.

"The more the Dutch parties make the English their spokesmen, the stronger their party becomes. You and Merriman could say things which, if said by any Dutchman, would fill the country with howls of 'treason!' If there were any other one man who seemed more likely than you to lead us to the ends we desire, I should earnestly wish you to stand down. I do not see any other man who can lead at the moment. The position has, in a sense, been forced on you. It's what the ancients called 'the voice of God'. It was Socrates' little demon and is undoubtedly in everyone who allows himself to be guided by it, One thing, however, is certain. When you act in obedience to it, you never regret, even though, in the eyes of the world, absolute failure may follow it." She laid aside her pen. Schreiner had already fallen sick from overwork. Public opinion called for stronger measures against the Transvaal, where President Kruger's secret police no longer bothered to hide the crimes they committed against the non-Dutch inhabitants. In the Cape, people talked openly of restoring Rhodes to his former glory, even before the enquiry into Jameson's Raid had reached a conclusion in London. Olive groaned at the thought, extinguished the lamp and went to bed, shaking her short-cropped head.

A few days before the end of the holidays an unexpected but welcome rain shower rolled in from the south, having managed to climb over the barrier of hills and reach the arid veldt. In less than two hours the drab buff plain became a blaze of variegated color. White starry kukumakranka, the

spiny stems of wild garlic, trailing clumps of bright yellow
volstruisdoring and delicate purple berkheya thistles blossomed everywhere. Olive sat on the stoep reading, another
lifelong habit she had acquired from her gifted well-read
mother. At the shallow pool the children splashed in the rain-
refreshed water, their games punctuated by screams whenever someone got pushed in. All the servant boys slept in the
shade of their grass-roofed huts. You had to be English or
mad to stay out in the midday sun. Even the mongrel farm
dogs had crawled under the stoep to doze away the hottest
hours. Tomorrow the flowers on the veldt would have faded
back to their uniform sun-baked buff color.

Olive put aside her book and gazed at the multicolored
landscape. It reminded her of a verse from the Bible, hardly
a verse she would have learnt from her Wesleyan missionary
father, the slow-moving heavily-bearded giant with the heart
of a child: 'Rise up my love, my fair one, and come away. For
lo, the winter is passed, the rain is over and gone. The flowers
appear on the earth and the sound of the turtledove is heard
in the land.' She realized that for poor South Africa this was
wishful thinking. The country had never been farther from
peace than it was at the present time. The turtledove sounded
more like a jackal. The sight of Louise kneeling at the drive-
side interrupted the thread of her thoughts. The little girl appeared equally moved by the sudden magical burst of bloom
on the arid veldt. She passed her chubby fingers among the
wild flowers with infinite precaution, in much the same way
as a pilgrim might touch the sacred relics of some long-for-
gotten martyr. When Olive next raised her head, the drive
was deserted and she turned back to her book.

Louise, however, had decided to do the forbidden and enter
the ostrich enclosure. The multicolored floral display urged
her on. In a flash she had crawled under the wire. Hardly
waiting to brush the dirt from her suit, she ran as fast as she
could away from the house. The blooms brushed her bare
legs. She stooped to pick armfuls of flowers she had never
seen outside picture books: deep yellow kouterbos, looking

like painted cauliflowers and covered with tiny insects; vivid pink wands of suurkanol, the upper stalks in bud and bursting to open before the moisture in the soil evaporated and plunged them back into a state of aestivation. She already saw in her mind's eye how they would look in her book of pressed flowers and how her father would congratulate her.

Suddenly tired by the dash across the undulating plain, Louise squatted by the remains of an abandoned termite hill. The hazy outline of the farm buildings shimmered in the distance. She screwed up her eyes against the glare and tried to focus on the eucalyptus grove. The distance prevented her from seeing any kind of activity and she began to have doubts about the wisdom of her escapade. She recalled Dumanie telling them once how an ostrich, if it kicked backwards, could bend an iron rail into a right angle. A movement in the blurred distance attracted her attention. A male ostrich, at least eight feet tall, had located her by the termite hill. She looked round for a place to hide. The treeless grassland rolled away in every direction. She could only think of a true story that had happened to her father on one of his official visits to a royal Zulu kraal. The court had assembled under an impressive baobab tree. During the interview, a snake had uncoiled itself from an overhead branch and swung between Henry and the Zulu Queen. Quite unmoved, she told him that the snake was the spirit of the dead King come to assist and to judge their guest's honesty. He had kept his head and remained cool and motionless. The snake had eventually hauled itself back into the branches.

Mumbling a confused medley of miscellaneous prayers, Louise did what ostriches were supposed to do and, making herself as small as possible, hid her head in her arms. Through a chink in her fingers she saw the mountain of black and white feathers approach with a hissing sound like a steam train.

Dumanie sent the children straight to bed after supper, instead of staying downstairs reading or drawing or doing jigsaw puzzles as usual. In the deserted drawing-room the farmer looked across at Olive.

"It seems that the child stayed in the same position for quite a long time; well over an hour in fact." He kept blowing out his red cheeks like a guinea pig. Olive controlled her annoyance.

"I can't understand how the girl escaped my attention," she repeated for the third time. "When I saw that she was no longer at the side of the track, I assumed she had returned to the others at the pond." She only hoped that Dumanie would keep the news from Henry Juta. He would be quick to accuse her of negligence. The girls, of course, would talk and probably embroider the tale into the bargain. Dumanie seized on the occasion of taking their minds off the delicate subject and talking on his favorite topic at the same time.

"The ostrich, you see Miss Schreiner, although he has keen eyesight, is very easily distracted. He seems to pass his entire life being distracted, sitting on a patch of sand, stretching his neck along the ground, as if he were peering at some distant object. Hence the belief that the ostrich buries its head in the sand. Quite untrue. From a distance you can see nothing but the body, which gives the impression that the head is buried. Luckily Louise adopted a position of dominated defeat—the head under the wing, so to speak." His wife started clicking her tongue and shaking her head.

"Give the child a good talking to. She's stubborn as a mule. Make her see she can't go causing distress in others just to satisfy her selfish whims." Dumanie sighed. The situation needed careful handling. It wasn't his role to educate somebody else's daughter. One of the farm boys had found Louise on his way back from repairing a boundary fence. Mrs. Dumanie had locked her in the bedroom and no one was allowed to visit her. It was the first time anyone had disobeyed the sacred 'marching orders'. The sisters had exchanged hurried whispers as Louise was led upstairs.

"Just think! You could have been killed!"

"Ripped to pieces by those awful claws!"

"Olive says God only saved you because He loves little children. So you were frightfully lucky!"

"But we love you too, so we won't tell the parents." Nanny had been allowed up to console her little 'missy' with a jug of iced lemon and countless warm hugs. Then Olive had to play the role of governess, a role she had played in a number of farms, often having to leave without warning because of the sexual predation of her male employers. Unfortunately she understood Louise. Sitting on the bed lecturing about obedience and about how grown-ups always knew better seemed more like hypocrisy than common sense. She possessed her own childhood memories of an African farm, where old Uncle Otto told tales in broken English. She saw herself crawling among the scattered stones of a kopje surrounded by the incessant rattle of cicadas. She remembered the burning zinc roof on the outbuilding, hot enough to fry an egg on, and the impenetrable blackthorn hedges that protected the kraal from nocturnal beasts; and always the immense magical call of the immutable veldt, dotted with brittle karroo bushes and isolated clumps of kangaroo thorn; and finally the African sky, blue and blazing and infinite.

CHAPTER . . .

4

The Enquiry into the Jameson Raid drew to an indeterminate close. Rhodes escaped serious sanctions. He freely admitted his responsibility for sending the doctor over the border, but evaded the more delicate issues by refusing to answer questions which might have incriminated third parties. Nobody appeared over-anxious to delve too deeply into the uncomfortable question of the Colonial Office's involvement. The only facts available consisted of those Rhodes condescended to supply. The investigation earned the cynical description of 'The Lying in State at Westminster'. With Johnny Grimmer in tow, Rhodes left England for a short tour of Europe and in mid-April his boat anchored in Table Bay.

For three days his jubilant supporters invaded Groote Schuur and showered him with congratulations. One evening a torch-light procession of artisans and tradesmen marched out from town to pledge their loyalty. By the time they reached the house, their numbers had exceeded five thousand. On the fourth day Rhodes returned from a ride up the mountain to see an unfamiliar female face among the waiting crowd on the stoep. Her sallow complexion, dark heavily-lidded eyes, thick very black hair and sensuous mouth gave her a gypsy air. She visibly monopolized his guests in a foreign accent and with numerous mistakes.

"What you require in this country," she was saying to Dr. Hans Sauer, one of the principal spokesmen of the Afrikaaner Bond in the Cape House of Assembly, "is a strong party, which has in its ranks all the strongest men as well as the most powerful, and which is not hindered by this present element of discord and infirmity." She looked directly out

67

of the corner of her eye at Rhodes as he climbed onto the stoep. Harry Currey hastily stepped forward to introduce the impetuous newcomer. He knew his boss's views on foreign women. In his opinion they couldn't live without constant intriguing and conspiracy.

Princess Catherine Radziwill barely acknowledged Rhodes' outstretched hand. In fact, she had recently broken her little finger, which made it painful to shake hands correctly. The princess had already caused a stir in Cape Town at a recent reception in honor of Sir Alfred Milner, the British High Commissioner, by refusing to stand up on Sir Alfred's entrance. She took her aristocratic heritage very seriously indeed.

Born as Countess Ekaterina Rzewuska in Saint Petersburg, her father, an arrogant Polish exile, had obtained the post of Military Governor from the Tsar for having ruthlessly crushed a rebellion of Polish peasants against their Russian overlords. A change of rulers brought Count Rzewuska into disfavor and Catherine's teens passed uneventfully on the huge country estates at Pohrebyszcze with its grim castle and thousands of suppressed serfs. The monotony of provincial life was broken only twice, when the Count attended the marriage of Alexander II to Princess Dagmar of Denmark and the following year he took his teenage daughter to Paris to visit her aunt Evelina de Balzac, the wife of the famous novelist. She had been married when they first met and their correspondence lasted many years before her husband died and she summoned Balzac to Poland to marry her.

Shortly after her fifteenth birthday Catherine learnt that her father had arranged her marriage to a Prussian Army officer of Polish-Lithuanian descent, Prince Wilhelm Radziwill. He whisked her away to the family palace in Berlin, rigidly superintended by the Prince's grandmother, Empress Louise of Prussia. Catherine rebelled. Eventually her intrigues, her reputation for sardonic wit, flirtatiousness and unorthodox political views forced her husband to leave Berlin and settle in Saint Petersburg. When Catherine showed no signs of controlling her tongue, a separation became inevitable. The Prince returned to Poland and Catherine reappeared in Paris and later in London.

"Surely you are not asking me to believe that you don't remember me, Mr. Rhodes?" Rhodes frowned. Why did everyone expect to be remembered? He searched frantically for some clue. A picture flashed into his mind: a dinner party three years ago given by Moberley Bell, the energetic manager of 'The Times.' Rhodes recalled the princess's tendency to express herself bluntly on delicate subjects. Her outspokenness had embarrassed him, but he had put it down to a regrettable foreign habit. He had been even more surprised the next day to receive a letter from the Princess, enclosing a coin she claimed had been carried by the 'great General Skobeleff', who had distinguished himself by his bravery in the Russo-Turkish War of 1887. In the letter she had written:

"You will be very much surprised to read these lines, but I have so often wished you at Jericho and heaped upon your head things that were the reverse of blessings, that now we have become acquainted, I feel I cannot let you sail for the Dark Continent without wishing you God speed with all my heart. I had imagined you quite different from what you are and fancied your only craving was money. I am sure now that I was mistaken, and that you only care for power in the good and true sense of the word."

Rhodes smiled covertly at the memory. There had even been rumors in London at the time that she had been enquiring into his eligibility as a potential husband. He bowed stiffly. Inclined to stoutness, her hair and eyes had not lost their black luster. Rhodes ploughed through the mob and retired to his study. For a while he wandered about the room, shifting about pieces of rare Delft china or even rarer old glass ornaments. More important things than Polish princesses preoccupied him. During his absence, vandals had broken into the grounds of Groote Schuur, lighting fires, cutting down trees and harming animals in his private zoo. This had dampened the victory of his triumphant return. To add insult to injury, William Schreiner, once his Attorney General and now the new Prime Minister, had moved house so as to live farther away from Groote Schuur. Jameson, never in very good health, was suffering in Holloway prison, condemned by the Lord Chief Justice to fifteen months. In fact, unknown to Rhodes, the sick doctor had been released for health reasons after serving only six months.

Rhodes paused to admire the latest addition to his china collection, brought back from Europe on the last trip. He caught sight of Gordon Le Sueur, one of his under-secretaries, passing the window and called him in to get his opinion. Le Sueur, who would later write one of the many biographies of Rhodes, could find little to say.

"Oh, I don't know. It's rather fine," he mumbled. Rhodes flew into a typical rage, his pale flaccid face going blotchy.

"I suppose," he snapped irritably, "if Jesus Christ were to ask you what you thought of heaven, you'd say: 'Oh, I don't know. It's rather fine!' You must think, Gordon. Remember, you must think! You must use your brains." Life in the Cape pleased him less and less. Something had gone. He needed to move north again, return to the veldt. Leading the opposition in the House didn't suit him at all. Most of the time he spent hurling veiled insults at poor Schreiner. It gave him little satisfaction to watch the struggling Prime Minister getting worked up at the back bench jeers. Sessions tended to be stormier than ever, nourished by a mounting feeling of uneasiness and general unrest. A few days before his last trip to England, Schreiner had publicly begged Rhodes 'to pass away for a period'. Did he really scare people that much? Or did they use him as a scapegoat, conveniently on hand to blame for the growing conviction that war with the Boer states could not be avoided much longer? Everyone talked endlessly on the subject. Yesterday's debate in the House had ended with Schreiner waving a wire from Marthinus Steyn, president of the Orange Free State. One of eleven children born on the family farm, Steyn had studied Law in Holland. Running under the colors of the pro-Dutch party, he had been elected President three years earlier. He attempted unsuccessfully to mediate between Paul Kruger and Lord Alfred Milner, the British High Commissioner. Schreiner had gone on and on about the wire being 'a message of peace', until Rhodes had lost his temper.

"On this side of the House," he insisted, "there is not one man, and I hope there are not many more than one on the other side, who does not long for peace. I tell honorable members that I shall not believe there will be no war until I hear the first shot fired!" Rhodes rose and walked out amid unrestrained applause. At the door Harry Currey touched his elbow.

"Time to go, sir," Rhodes sighed. He had forgotten the reception at the Mount Nelson Hotel. Had he been free to choose, he would have preferred a good book in the quiet of his study.

Half an hour later he lumbered into the hotel reception lounge, conspicuously massive and bovine with his white flaccid face and heavy-lidded blue eyes. He stopped to chat with Sir Henry and Lady Juta. At least they hadn't moved house to get farther away from him! He learnt that their baby son, Jan, had been seriously ill, the two eldest girls were still happy at boarding-school in England and that Louise seemed only interested in acting and climbing trees.

In one corner of the room, seated in the large bay window with its view over Table Bay he noticed a broad middle-aged man of average height with a remarkably short neck. He wore a waist-length brown coat, very full trousers and held a broad-brimmed flat brown hat on his knees. He peered at his audience from behind the thickest pair of spectacles Rhodes had ever seen.

"England is a wonderful land!" the visitor exclaimed. "It's the most marvelous of all the foreign countries I've ever been in. It's made up of trees and fields and mud and the gentry!" Rhodes' sober face lit up as he recognized Rudyard Kipling, the famous Anglo-Indian author of 'The Jungle Book', and one of the most popular writers in English at the time. Except for an Athenium dinner in April, they had not met for six years. A lot of water had passed under the bridge since then. He strode over.

"Kipling! I had no idea you were in the Cape. Let's go away and talk. Where are you staying?" Kipling took off his spectacles and polished them. He stared blindly at the carpet.

"Oh, we've found a very nice place at Newlands, a boarding-house, very simple," he replied. Outside the hotel windows the dazzling afternoon sun reflected off the sea's smooth surface and the whitewashed walls of the harbor buildings. Only the short-sighted author seemed immune to the glare. Rhodes shielded his eyes.

"How do you like our African sun?" he asked. "Better than Torquay, eh?" After living four years in Vermont with his American wife, Carrie Balestier, Kipling had hurriedly brought his family back to England because of rising anti-British sentiment in America, which had culminated in his brother-in-law's arrest for threatening him with physical harm. They settled in a hillside home overlooking the sea in Torquay. England held emotionally mixed memories for Kipling. Following the custom in British India, Kipling and his three-year old sister, Alice, had found themselves living for six years with foster parents. He recalled this time with horror, but wondered ironically if the combination of cruelty and neglect he experienced there at the hands of Captain and Mrs. Holloway might not have hastened the onset of his literary life. The calculated religious and scientific torture made him pay attention to the lies he soon found it necessary to tell, and this, he presumed, was the foundation of all literary effort.

"I never told anyone how I was being treated," he remembered. "Badly-treated children tell little more than animals. They have a clear notion of what they are likely to get if they betray the secrets of the prison before they are clear of it! My sister fared better. Mrs. Holloway seemed to be hoping that Trix would eventually marry her son."

Rudyard Kipling was a man worthy of Rhodes' own imperialist philosophy. George Orwell called him 'a prophet

of British imperialism' He was universally recognized as an
incomparable, if controversial, interpreter of the empire experience. He had traveled the world. His father, Lockwood
Kipling, held the post of professor of architectural sculp-
ture in Bombay. His vivacious mother earned the praises of
the Viceroy: "Dullness and Mrs. Kipling cannot exist in the
same room." The writer had already visited South Africa, on
the lookout for a clement climate to winter in. He had been
to Australia, New Zealand, twice to Japan and lived for four
years on his wife's property in Vermont. Like Rhodes he pro-
fessed to be a lover of peace. The persistent damp drizzle
of Devonshire depressed him. Fundamentally he was a nomadic colonial. His heart lay at the foot of a Union Jack flut-
tering against a tropical sky.

"How are you coping with the fatherland?" Rhodes enquired, as they settled into the plush armchairs with their
drinks. Rhodes' intervention had driven off the group of admirers. They both felt the immense satisfaction of having
won a few seconds of peace. Kipling smiled mournfully.

"Eight damp months; rain, sea fog and mildew!" he complained, his bushy mustache quivering with indignation. Recently he had taken his wife house-hunting nearer London.
They had discovered a suitable property in Sussex, but the
owners didn't want to sell. Called 'Batemans', the well-built
square Jacobean house sat in a lonely valley at the bottom of
a steep lane a mile from a small village. Kipling paused to sip
his drink. Rhodes looked at the drifting crowd of guests, the
oily tide of cocktail humanity, ebbing and flowing across the
red Turkish carpet like an antediluvian slug. He shuddered.

"I don't suppose we can decently leave yet."

"No, I don't suppose so," agreed Kipling, blinking behind
his thick lenses. Carrie had refused to come with him. At
least she had the children as an excuse. After seven years'
marriage and three children their marital relationship was
no longer as light-hearted and spontaneous. They remained
loyal to each other but seemed to have fallen into set roles.
Kipling admitted that marriage had taught him 'the tougher

virtues, such as humility, restraint, order and forethought.' He had accepted the invitation to the reception out of curiosity, in the hope that something might crop up to excite him. He had heard the guest of honor, the opera singer Emma Albani, give a recital in San Francisco ten years before. It remained conspicuous in his memory only for the over-sentimental rendering of 'Home Sweet Home' that ended the concert. Born in Quebec as Marie-Louise-Emma-Cécile Lajeunesse, Albani had become the first Canadian opera singer to reach world renown. Her stage career had now ended but she still toured the world giving recitals.

The two men watched her on the far side of the lounge receiving the homage of her admirers. Her figure, remarkably well-proportioned for a prima donna, remained presentable. She wore a white velvet dress that broadened at the bottom and fell in a wide fan-shaped circle to one side. Decorated with half-closed olive green laurel leaves like miniature harps, it matched perfectly the brilliant white stole, draped carelessly over the chair behind her. Henry and Helen Juta had managed to get her alone for a moment. Both talented musicians who encouraged all their children to play an instrument or sing, it might have amused them to know that one day their own Louise would go to Paris to study opera and even sing duets with Enrico Caruso. Rhodes studied the trio and chuckled.

"It's a rare sport being cornered by a robust prima donna past her prime," he whispered. "A fat duchess is better. First I tell her what I think of her. She smiles and shakes her head. I go one better and give out a few oaths. She begins to gush. I blaspheme. She laughs. I become Rabelaisian. She guffaws. I curse. She fawns. There's no limit to her endurance." He burst out into his alarming falsetto laugh, so surprising coming from such a huge man. As always heads turned in his direction. William Schreiner sidled in with Hofmeyr, skirted the wall farthest from Rhodes and retired to a corner table.

"Poor old Willie," muttered Rhodes. "His days as Prime Minister are numbered, I fear. There's going to be war and it'll topple him." Kipling nodded towards the prima donna.

"I hear that Madame Albani sang in Johannesburg last week. They told her not to sing 'God Save the Queen' at the end of her recital."

"Did she?"

"Of course!" They both laughed. Rhodes got slowly to his feet.

"Let's go and do our duty," he said with a groan, running a hand through his tousled fair hair. Outside, a rosy vesperal tint illuminated the sandstone cliffs below Signal Hill. Sky-wheeling gulls circled the port. The Atlantic swell hissed in the shingle along the weed-draped sea wall under the hotel windows. Rhodes lumbered across the room. He felt feverish.

"Tomorrow and tomorrow and tomorrow," he mumbled and bent to kiss the proffered hand in front of him.

The following afternoon found the same people gathered for a piano recital in 'Mon Desir'. Liszt's eighth Hungarian Rhapsody drew to an end and Emma Albani followed each note from memory. There had always been music in her life. Born within earshot of the roaring rapids on the River Richelieu, its music had competed with that of her father, a Breton organist. He had immigrated to Canada and brought with him the austere mystery of French cathedrals. When he stopped playing his hand-built organ in the house, the waters along the lakeshore sang. Emma had gone on singing; first in New York music halls to earn enough money to study, then in Paris with the operatic tenor Louis Duprez, who had been personally chosen by Donizetti to sing Edgardo in the first performance of 'Lucia di Lammermoor' in Naples and finally in Rome under Francesco Lamperti, perhaps the greatest singing teacher of the century. Since her début at Messina, Emma Albani had sung all over the world.

On either side of their guest, the Juta couple followed the pianist's hands over the keyboard. The open windows onto the croquet lawn allowed the faint rasp of a hoe on the gravel to compete with the music and Henry made a mental note to reprimand the gardener afterwards. To his left the four girls sat stiffly erect on dining-room chairs, aware of their father's eyes turned in their direction from time to time.

Their mother's education fitted her to be the best judge of the playing. All those heart-breaking hours at the piano in the Paris hotel suite with the tantalizing hum from the boulevard below the window to taunt her. She had practiced her ubiquitous scales while the Parisians mourned the death of Léon Gambetta and the dissolution of the Jesuits. During her adolescence and until her marriage to Harry Juta, life was an immutable six month cycle of Karlsbad for the cure, Paris for music and clothes. If marriage put an end to Murdoch Tait's eagle eye, it didn't put an end to music. Most evenings at 'Mon Desir' echoed to melodious sounds. Mr. Pieris, a talented Dutch musician, arrived every day to give violin or piano lessons to the Juta girls.

Emma Albani had a special reason to be haunted by the piece the pianist had chosen. It took her back twelve years to a London still aghast at the violent murder by the Irish of Gladstone's nephew, sent over to Dublin to negotiate a settlement on the Irish Land Act. Amid the confusion and outrage, Liszt had arrived on a short visit. Albani had assisted at his reception in the Grafton Gallery. The following evening she had sung the title role in his Oratorio 'Saint Elizabeth' at the St. James Hall. A year later the enigmatic Hungarian abbé died at his daughter's home in Bayreuth.

The rhapsody ended. At eighteen, the young pianist had stopped off briefly at Cape Town on his way back to London from a world tour ending in Australia. Of Russian origin, Mark Hambourg's family had moved to London in 1889 as refugees from the Tsarist regime and taken British nationality. At eleven he was touring the provinces, the family being too poor to turn down such opportunities. He soon became tired of 'little old ladies wanting to kiss me. I permitted them to do so only in exchange for a large box of chocolates.' With his father and two younger brothers, he gave recitals of chamber music.

Hambourg left the piano and walked confidently over to his hostess. Perhaps he had in mind the reaction of Bernard Shaw after a performance of Bach: "This Russian lad might

astonish the world some day." Helen Juta drew his attention
to some detail in his interpretation and the young pianist
nodded an acknowledgment of the compliment.

"In the steps of the master," he insisted. His playing had
been greatly influenced by his father, a professor at the Moscow Conservatory and a pupil of Anton Rubinstein. Despite
his years in England, his voice still held strong traces of the
old Slav accent.

"Wonderful playing, Mr. Hambourg," exclaimed Emma
Albani, shaking his hand as though she hoped that the magic
in the long fingers might pass by some osmotic process into
her own ailing vocal chords. "It might have been the Abbé
himself playing," she added.

"You are too kind, and unjustly so," he retorted. His youthful naivety and lack of experience had not taught him to
mimic the conventional indifference of all great artists. Although he had made his début in Moscow at the age of ten,
Mark Hambourg had always relied on the paternal wing to
protect him. With his two brothers they formed a compact
musical unity that needed no false allure. It would soon end.
Jan had started taking violin lessons with Emile Sauret, the
French violinist who had actually performed sonatas with
Liszt at the piano. Boris would go to Frankfurt to the study
the cello.

Helen Juta gathered her guests together and led them out
into the garden to the waiting table on the lawn. As the group
emerged from the French windows, the butler cast a last
look over the crystal dishes of syllabub, the champagne fruit
cups, the numerous varieties of ice-cream and the tempting
jug of iced coffee. In the kitchen he had tasted the syllabub,
a dish of whipped cream mixed with wine and solidified with
gelatin. Cook had overdone the wine, which would displease
Henry Juta who would inevitably blame the butler.

The heat of the day waned to a disquieting nagging in the
back of the memory. Cooling air drifted up from the flats. A
rising sea breeze lingered among the oak leaves and swayed
the topmost branches of the pines. It breathed the balmy

scent of the acacia and minaret bushes. Only Renée had obtained permission to take tea with the adults. At fourteen, she already showed an intellectual precocity in advance of her years. Her sisters knelt in the nursery window and observed. They noticed the young Russian pianist try to escape from the famous singer. She looked more like the duchess in 'Alice in Wonderland' and wouldn't stop talking. Grandmother Juta had started her third champagne cup. Their father had taken one of his legal colleagues aside to talk court business. What a bore!

Louise yawned. She regretted the lovely teas they used to have with 'Uncle' Jan Smuts, before he left Cape Town and moved up to Johannesburg. At first the young lawyer and political journalist had supported Cecil Rhodes, but like so many others, the Jameson Raid had destroyed his confidence and he had moved to the Transvaal to become a state attorney. He worked for a peaceful solution to the Uitlander question, persuading President Kruger to make considerable concessions to the British. When negotiations collapsed, however, he published a vitriolic attack on British policy in South Africa.

Louise missed walks with the barrister looking for flowers. Born into an Afrikaner farming family in Cape colony, Jan Smuts possessed an enviable knowledge of Cape wild life and particularly the flora. He impressed upon the Juta girls the unawareness among the general public of the beauty and wealth around them.

"Our Cape plants belong to a flora which is unique and to which a great deal of mystery attaches," he explained, as they rambled over the lower slopes of Table Mountain. "A large number of plant families are found nowhere else in the world or have only distant relatives in countries like Australia." A wealth of information, Smuts never allowed a visit to pass without teaching them something new. He informed them about scientists like Joseph Hooker and Charles Darwin, who believed in a lost continent under the Indian Ocean, Antarctica being the only remaining vestige. The northern limit of this lost continent may have stretched as far north as the Cape peninsular, a kind of utopia, and a happy land, where people of different races could live together in harmony with nature.

"Surely there's nothing more wonderful in the world than this land, set between two seas, girdled by mountains, with its clear benign air by day, its starlit heavens by night and its rich heritage of floral life; sometimes even more than one can bear." Suddenly he had ceased coming. Their father told the girls that he had gone north to fill the post of Transvaal attorney. He came south no more.

The nursery door opened. Grandmother Juta looked in. She always found a moment to come upstairs and visit her grandchildren, all very attached to her. The same couldn't be said for grandmother Tait. Helen Juta's mother possessed a way of talking, probably copied from her bearish banker husband that made the girls wish they had sunk below the earth. Henry Juta's mother was different. Born among the Moselle Hills of the Rhineland in the historic 10th century town of Trier, she had retained much of her German mannerisms and accent. The mystery of her family past intrigued the girls most, particularly as Henry Juta always lost his temper if the subject were mentioned and refused to discuss the black sheep of the family. Grandmother Louise's brother, dead for over sixteen years, had been exiled from Germany for writing a book prophesying a classless society in which laws and government would take second seat. Great-uncle Karl Marx had died in London, very poor, very arrogant and full of hatred. Anyone who mentioned Uncle Karl in front of Henry Juta had dropped a sizeable brick. He found his uncle's political views unacceptably revolutionary. His assertion that the victory of the working class must be followed by repression of the former ruling class, Sir Henry's, until the last vestiges of the old order were extinguished, made Henry Juta shudder. Marx predicted a classless, collectivist order in which social product was distributed according to needs and in which the state and the concept of economic value had lost their functions. Two skeletons hid in the cupboard and Henry Juta forbade all allusion to them: Uncle Karl's third daughter, Henry's cousin, had committed suicide and the family had Jewish origins.

"Of course he wasn't Jewish!" he would thunder. Louise often wanted to ask Nanny how it changed a person to be Jewish. Grandmother Louise didn't look any different. She had a faded photo of Uncle Karl on her dressing table and he really did look a little different with his extraordinary mass of hair and enormous beard. Not at all like Papie. Perhaps Grandmother Louise was so nice because she was Jewish. So Louise listened to this sweet old lady and from her slow carefully-chosen words tried to reach her own conclusion.

"Now zen, geliebt child. Vat haf you been learning dis veek?" She pulled up her chair at the table. Her gnarled beringed fingers swept away the clutter of toy animals that waited impatiently to be put back into the huge Noah's Ark in the middle of the carpet. Louise stood obediently at her side, breathing in the slightly sour scent of her old body mixed with jasmine toilet water. She could hardly admit that today she had learnt nothing, which was the truth. She had spent most of her 'school hour' sitting in the corner making designs on the wallpaper with her tongue. Could she remember one of the Shakespeare verses she had learnt for her father? Possibly, but she didn't feel like it. Grandmother Louise smiled.

"Say me vat you haf learnt for your papie," she coaxed. Louise put her hands behind her back, as she had been taught, and took a deep breath. She watched Jan out of the corner of her eye. The little boy sat on a stool under the window daubing paint over a large sheet of blue paper.

"How like a winter hath my absence been from thee, the pleasure of the fleeting year. What freezings have I felt, what dark days seen; what old December's bareness everywhere." The old German lady threw up her hands in admiration. It hardly mattered that Louise understood little of what she recited. The child was obviously gifted. She had not spoken automatically like a parrot, but with feeling; a gift for acting she had inherited from someone. Other voices from seventy years ago echoed the lines: "Meine Ruh' ist hin, mein Hertz ist schwer." She saw another little girl in long plaited pigtails reciting her lessons to her Jewish father, a lawyer from Trier with a keen interest in philosophy who had recently had all his family baptized as Protestants. She turned her attention to Jan.

"And vat are you painting zere, Jan? Come here and show me, child." Jan trotted over with the sodden sheet of paper. From a blaze of spontaneous color appeared what might have been a beach with purple hills rising to the towering table-top mountain that dominated their lives. What a family she had married into! Her eye caught sight of something near the top of the painting.

"The sun. Zere is not too much red in it? You don't sink? You see it like that. So! Perhaps zere is not then." Below the nursery windows the guests returned from tea on the lawn for the second half of the recital. Nanny arrived to fetch the younger girls. They trouped with military precision along the oak-paneled passage to the head of the ornamental staircase. They could hear Emma Albani telling her hostess how American audiences always appreciated her singing so much, particularly her interpretation of Gilda in Verdi's 'Rigoletto' at the Metropolitan in New York. Her husband was later to make some very unwise investments and reduce the couple to near poverty, obliging the prima donna to sing in music halls.

Servants hurriedly removed the tables on the lawn and closed the French windows. A crepuscular silence invaded the darkening park. A brilliant black and yellow oriole glided in over the pine tops. It alighted onto a branch, uttering sporadic harsh cat-like calls. The sound spurred the sparrows on the roof slates into a burst of frenzied chatter that ceased as suddenly as it had begun, the birds seemingly embarrassed by the silent shroud of night that had caught them unaware and vulnerable.

The following weekend the entire Juta family descended to the coast at St. James. Shortly after the birth of his first daughter, Henry Juta had purchased a villa there to use as a weekend retreat. A fashionable seaside resort on False Bay, St. James rocked to the pounding Pacific breakers on the Koeelberg, whose high cliffs plunged deep into the water. A long curving sandy beach formed the northern shore. 'False Bay' earned its name from sixteenth century sailors returning from the east who confused it with Table Bay. Opposite the Juta villa, a mile off-shore rose Seal Island, the main breeding site for the Cape Fur Seal. The seals attracted many Great White Sharks, famous for the manner in which they breached the surface of the water while attacking seals, sometimes jumping entirely out of the ocean.

The various members of the family viewed these weekend expeditions with different degrees of enthusiasm. Henry Juta cherished the opportunity of spending a few days on the rocks with a fishing line, often with Willie Schreiner, when the new Prime Minister could get out of playing cricket with the youngsters on the grassy strip between the station and the beach. Angling from the rocky shores on either side of the bay could be dangerous. 'Killer waves' rose up without warning and swept the sandstone ledges well above the high tide mark. Scores of fishermen had drowned over the years and this was a constant cause of anguish for Helen Juta, who had to watch her husband knee-deep on a weedy ledge with his fishing rod. Sometimes he would pay a Malay fisherman to row him out into the bay to pit his skill against the larger fish. This scared her even more. The 'killer waves' wreaked havoc with sailing craft and some of the biggest sharks ever seen had been spotted in those waters.

Of the five Juta children, only the youngest, Jan and Louise, shared their father's passion for these seaside weekends. They combed the sandy strip of beach for shells or scrambled among rock pools in search of sea anemones or stranded starfish. Helen Juta and her elder daughters showed less enthusiasm. They criticized the lack of habitual amenities and home comforts. The salt wind damaged their fine dresses and burnt their delicate skin. They had to depend entirely on nature for entertainment. They spent their time trying to think of excuses for a rapid return to 'Mon Desir'.

Cecil Rhodes' fantasy had also led him into buying a property on False Bay. Fantasy, because the property he chose differed so radically from Groote Schuur. As a retreat, or more accurately a place of shelter where he could breathe more freely, Rhodes chose a primitive iron-roofed shack. No doubt it made him feel closer to his beloved veldt. The hut nestled under the Hangklip, squeezed between the rocky crag and the beach with the road and the railway between him and the sea. A low verandah made of wire mosquito meshing covered the façade. It looked like a series of dilapidated rabbit hutches stuck onto the front of the shack as an afterthought. In comparison, the Juta villa, a substantial white two-storey clapboard home with green shutters, passed for a palace. The indefatigable pounding of ocean surf rocked them to sleep every night and woke them every morning. From the front porch they followed the whole sweep of Danger Beach right round the point to Clovelly.

To inaugurate the weekend, on the first morning Henry Juta sacrificed his planned fishing trip and took the family along the rocky coast to Strandfontain. The isolated fishing village lay at the far end of the Cape's longest sand beach, an immense stretch of dune-fringed shore running for half False Bay to the foot of the Blousteenberg Hills in the north. The entire coastline lacked roads and the beach provided the sole access to the village. The family dressed for the occasion while servants prepared the picnic in the kitchen. The Malay driver brought the ox cart to the front of the villa. The cumbersome but remarkably sturdy vehicle creaked to a stop. The two white oxen stood shoulder to shoulder with bovine indifference as the driver checked the yoke.

While he waited for his wife and daughters, Henry Juta strolled over the railway tracks in search of William Schreiner. He found him, dressed in an old pair of white cricket flannels and a battered boater hat, mending a fishing line.

"It's all wretched," he complained in reply to his friend's cheerful greeting. "Wherever the work or the influence of Rhodes comes to light, it leaves a nasty taste in the mouth." The upper corner of his mouth twitched and he toyed nervously with his ample graying beard. The latest government crisis had broken over the delivery of munitions to the Orange Free State, the second autonomous Boer state north of the Orange River. Tensions between Britain and the Transvaal had increased and war was now openly envisaged. Rhodes and the opposition bench demanded to know why Schreiner had authorized arms and ammunition to transit through to the Boer states. They accused him of treachery; a colonial Prime Minister who let his country's potential enemies arm themselves for war against his own soldiers. Schreiner gesticulated wildly.

"Damn it all, Buddie!" he exclaimed. "This is a time of peace. The Orange Free State is, under the Convention, entitled to get these arms and ammunition. For me to withhold them might bring things to the brink of war. It would be seriously embarrassing to the Imperial Government in London, and it would be absolutely illegal!" The voice of the lawyer spoke. He applied the law to the letter, unlike others in his profession who had learnt the rules merely to be able to manipulate them later. It reminded Henry Juta of something a barrister colleague in London had told him: "Good heavens, Juta! Didn't you know? Today, the only honest man is the idiot!"

Schreiner laid aside his fishing line and started pacing the dusty cricket pitch, tossing a ball in his hands. Henry Juta fell into step with him.

"The responsibility rests with London," he argued. "It is for Whitehall to say whether it will be more dangerous and more damaging to allow this ammunition to go forward or to bring things to a crisis by taking an unfriendly attitude and stopping the shipment." His cool common sense always calmed Schreiner. Behind them the cricket match had started and he bent down to stop a wild ball about to bounce off the pitch into the rocks. He tossed it back to the youthful wicket keeper. Henry Juta sighed. His friend's naivety disturbed him. President Steyn's attempts at a peaceful settlement and his mediation with Paul Kruger failed to hide the reality. The fire had already been lit by Jameson's stupid raid into Transvaal. Schreiner's stubborn sticking to the word of the law reminded him of Thomas Moore's blind faith in 'the thickets of the law', that had led him down the shortest path to the scaffold.

He saw his family ready at last and waiting by the ox cart. The younger children had already clambered into the back under the canvas. Nanny fussed about handing in the picnic baskets. Henry Juta took his friend by the elbow and they walked back over the railways tracks.

"We're going to Strandfontain," he said. "Shell-hunting. Why don't you come with us, Buddie? Do you good." Schreiner only hesitated a second.

"Nothing I'd like better, but..." The sentence remained unfinished. They both knew that in an hour or two the Prime Minister would be back in Cape Town behind his desk, caught up once more in the death struggle between London and Johannesburg, a struggle that left him powerless, a mere pawn to be shifted around the chessboard of imperial politics.

The creaking cart moved off along the immense curve of dazzling white sand, the oxen straining at the yoke, the driver skillfully steering them onto the harder patches and away from zones where the wind had drifted the dune sand onto the beach. A light land breeze rippled the transparent turquoise water in the bay. Seal Island rose haze-hidden and pale purple on the sky line. A faint ring of white foam curled round the base where the ocean swell washed over the rocks. Small groups of brown and white petrels fluttered above the water on their long wedge-shaped wings. The September sun had brought the dunes to life. Bright green lizards lazed in sheltered hollows. A leopard toad peered at them from a clump of saltbush, blinked and dug itself back under the sand.

At Muizenberg they passed close to Rhodes' shack, where he was to die in only two years. A line of colorful cabins bordered the shell-scattered beach. The well-preserved ruins of a small customs fort built in 1673 had resisted the winter gales. It remained as a reminder of the battle fought here, which had allowed the English to occupy the Cape. Beyond the fishing village the breeze-driven water of Sandvlei Lake mirrored the cloudless sky. Two skiffs darted to and fro on the ruffled surface, white sails veering in the wind like Chinese kites. The ox cart splashed through the stream at East Beach, the massive wooden wheels carving ruts in the soft sand. For the last long lap they could savor the wild loneliness of the dune-fringed shore with the pounding ocean surf on one side and the monotonous marshy salt flats on the other. In places the dune had been colonized by carpets of broad strap-shaped sea squills, the tall cylindrical spikes of white flowers growing leafless from the sand. The colored fishermen sometimes collected the huge swollen bulbs for medicinal purposes, as a treatment for heart disease.

Today's outing aimed at collecting the maximum number of nautilus shells possible. The early season made the task doubtful. The plankton beds on which the mollusks fed remained far out to sea still. Henry Juta gave the children a lesson, as he always did.

"There are two kinds of nautilus; the pearly or chambered nautilus, found in the south-west Pacific and the paper nautilus, the one we find here on our Cape beaches, the nautilus argonauta. He lives near the surface and feeds on plankton, microscopic organic life forms floating in the ocean. He inhabits a shell cradled by flaps in which he lays eggs. When you see him sailing with the arm flaps extended like sails, he looks like a ship. That's why in Latin he's called 'argonauta', from the ancient Greek word for 'sailor'." The older girls pretended not to listen. They had to put up with enough schoolroom lectures during the week, but to Louise her father was an admirable hive of information. Nothing seemed to escape his attention. The smallest detail unfolded before her eyes as a whole new field of knowledge. They passed an isolated stand of oak trees.

"Who knows what these trees are?" he asked,

"Oaks, of course," replied Renée disdainfully.

"Yes, but what oaks?" continued her father.

"Does it really matter what oaks they are, Henry?" interceded Helen Juta, defending her daughter's defiant reaction. Ignoring her remark, Henry Juta launched into a botanical litany about the different species of oak tree; the valonia oak used in tanning, the holm oak for ship building and feeding pigs, the cork oak for wine bottles and the kermes oak, "from which we obtain two dyes, a beautiful red dye from the dried bodies of an insect that lives on the leaves and a black dye from the bark." His explanation ceased suddenly as the regular swaying rhythm of the wagon changed. The oxen had begun to sink in a zone of waterlogged sand. Joined by the solid yoke, they struggled against each other. The heavy wooden wagon started to tilt dangerously as the wheels on one side sank into the subsiding sand. Henry Juta leaned out of the back and studied the situation. The wagon boy should have seen the danger and steered clear of it.

"Now just sit still," he said calmly. "We'll be out of this in a minute." His unruffled voice never betrayed the alarm he felt at the potentially perilous situation. The panicking oxen reared and wrestled with the increasingly tilted wagon. Brenda only just saved herself from being thrown onto the floor. She avoided the topple by clinging to Renée.

"Well, really!" she complained. "I do think that the boy might.." Henry Juta coughed loudly and raised a finger to silence her. For a few seconds the fear transmitted by the oxen and their frantic driver made itself felt. Then with a final shudder the wagon rose from the quicksand, creaked a few yards onto firmer ground and came to a stop. No one spoke. Only Henry Juta appreciated the danger they had escaped. On the tide line the breakers continued to thunder as if nothing had happened. Offshore the petrels continued to flutter and hop over the waves. Henry Juta climbed down. The exhausted oxen stood shivering and shocked. The wagon boy sat perched on his seat and stared stupidly at the ground.

Henry Juta sent him off to cut brushwood from the dunes to lay under the wheels until he was sure they had left the danger zone. Behind the wagon it looked as though an army of tanks had driven through. They would have to find another way round on the return trip.

Despite their father's pessimistic forecast, on arriving at their destination the children saw a whole fleet of nautilus shells approaching the beach on the crests of the incoming waves. Against the deep blue sea the floating shells appeared even whiter with their sails up and prows set straight for the shore. Louise and Jan lost no time. They waded into the water, communicating with each other through a complex sound language they had invented to indicate the discovery of a particularly interesting specimen. Shells with scarlet 'fans' they prized most for the startling contrast they made with the blinding white sand. Whole undamaged shells with pearly chambers and reddish-brown flame markings came second.

By lunchtime with the sun at its zenith the two shell-gathers had trouble keeping on their feet and staggered back to the rest of the family, sedately seated on rugs under a feathery tamarisk tree. The slender spikes of delicate pink flowers quivered in the rising breeze. The noontime heat made the bluish-gray leaves perspire and from time to time tiny drops of water fell on the dozing girls below. Henry Juta had walked into Strandfontain village to visit an old fisherman, an acquaintance of long date. Louise set about tackling the problem of how to transport the precious shells back to 'Mon Desir' and into the 'museum' without breaking any of them. The museum, a small green pavilion in the pine wood, had been built for the two younger Jutas to satisfy their natural mania for collecting things. The pavilion contained shelves full of pot fragments, old coins and worthless miscellaneous items of very relative antiquity that Mr. Sclater had recuperated from the Municipal Museum storerooms and had been earmarked for the rubbish bin. Neatly-labeled glass cases held collections of butterflies pinned on card, a grass snake in a bottle and two long-tailed reddish-brown stuffed warblers perched on a bit of branch. Coral and various shells decorated the walls among long necklaces of bright green sea eggs, meticulously sorted so that the longest hung in the middle and tapered off progressively to the sides. Louise took charge of decoration and antiquity. The six-year old Jan headed the Natural history department. Once a week he was taken into Cape Town and given lessons in taxidermy from the curator's German assistant.

On his return from the village, Henry Juta examined the morning's discoveries with paternal pride. Jan had found an unusual voluta shell half-buried among weed on the tide line. Shaped like a narrow pointed turban and in perfect condition, dark ochre streaks overlayed the yellow nacre. The wagon boy, recovered from his frightening encounter with the quicksand, prepared a fire in the sand and they grilled the fresh fish he had bought in the village. Some distance away a knot of native fishermen sat in a circle mending their nets in the fierce sun. They had told Henry Juta about a stranded whale on the beach a mile to the east and most of the other fishermen had run over to see what could be salvaged. All the children except Renée scrambled to their feet.

"Do let's go and have a look!" they cried. Their father smiled mischievously and looked over at the driver, still busy with kindling the fire from bunches of salt bush.

"He don't smell too good now," the boy remarked philosophically. "It's two days he bin stuck up on that beach." He made a strange humming noise, perhaps intended to imitate the cloud of bluebottles certainly active around the rotting carcass.

"And you, child?" Henry Juta turned to Louise, still sorting shells with Jan under the tree.

"Really, Daddy!" protested Renée, her impudent little nose lifted as though the stench had already reached her delicate nostrils. "Do you really think it's necessary to Lou's education to stare at a smelly old whale?" She looked at Brenda for support, but her sister had heard nothing, being absorbed in her book. Henry Juta tried to look stern.

"Come now, Renée!" he expostulated. "Experience is the child of thought and thought is the child of action. A far greater man than I came to that conclusion." He signaled to the boy to bring the wagon closer. At the end of the beach a wheeling cloud of gulls rose and fell. The children could even make out the milling black bodies, a long line of human ants trailing from the water's edge into the dunes.

The whale did in fact smell frightfully bad. An adult fin whale, it had perhaps been thrown up on the steeply-shelving beach by a rogue wave. Probably eighty feet long, the dark upper body contrasted markedly with its pure white underside. An army of crabs crawled over its yellow-streaked flanks. A squabbling multitude of sea birds vied for the best places amid a cacophony of harsh bugle-like calls and incessant cackling. Much of one side had already vanished. An uninterrupted procession of half-clad natives transported hastily-cut hunks of blubber in buckets, boxes and wooden crates back to the village. Three totally naked men kept the column supplied. Knee-deep in bloody gore, they butchered the whale with bush knives. Seemingly immune to the overpowering stench and the millions of flies buzzing round their heads, their powerful black bodies glistened with sweat and putrefying fat.

Curiosity can soon be satisfied, however, and even Louise's first glimpse of a naked man could not compete with the smell of the dead whale. A sad sight, it brought to mind a line from the Bible: 'How are the mighty fallen'. Soon the wonderful marine giant would be little more than a trail of blood across the sand and a mountain of bleached bones to be washed away by the next high tide. They drove back in silence, strangely disappointed with themselves. A pin-point plume of blue smoke rose from the camp fire. The twin ruts of the wagon wheels stretched away into the hazy distance, like the normic skein of life they had only just begun to understand.

5

"I suppose you do realize, Rhodes, that if you keep on robbing nests in order to eat the eggs, the penguin will soon be extinct in South Africa," declared Dr. Jameson with a yawn, prodding at the penguin egg omelet on his plate. "Not that you'd give a damn, anyway," he added, putting down his knife and fork. The Scottish doctor had only recently returned to Cape Town. The British authorities had released him from prison on the grounds of ill health, probably a more convenient way of ridding the country of an embarrassing prisoner. Still close friends with the ex-Prime Minister, he acknowledged his role in the ruin of Rhodes' flourishing political career.

Opposite him at table, Princess Radziwill seemed quite at home; too much at home, thought Jameson, as he watched her black shifty eyes scanning the rustic room in the Muizenberg shack. Such a sad contrast with the elaborate elegance of Groote Schuur! She scrutinized Rhodes sitting at her right hand side. She reminded Jameson of a Diana with her quiver full of erotic arrows. Where were the open-throated hounds? Catherine Radziwill had set her sights and with the stubborn perseverance of her clan would not relinquish the prey easily. Totally separated from her husband and a failure in the world of journalism, where she had hoped to make her mark, the Polish princess had set about spinning her web round Rhodes.

Jameson snorted with contempt at his friend's frailty. The woman was a hopeless case. On the voyage back from England in the 'Scot', Catherine had invited herself to sit at the reserved table Rhodes shared with the son of Lord Metcalf, a past Governor-General of India and later Canada. She monopolized the conversation with gossip about her divorce, implying that she would soon be free to remarry. She hung on Rhodes' every word and went out of her way to flatter him. She followed him about the deck, cornering him against the railing at every opportunity. The climax came inevitably one afternoon after the passage of Saint Helena. The couple sat side by side in deck chairs. Suddenly the princess gasped convulsively and fainted on Rhodes' lap. The look of abject helplessness on his friend's face, as they waited for someone to fetch smelling salts, had disgusted the doctor.

Back in the Cape, Catherine had rented a villa on the beach. Hardly a day passed without her stout pixy figure being seen strolling down the dusty lane past Rhodes' 'cottage'.

The servant cleared the plates away and they moved into the collection of rabbit hutches known as the 'verandah' for dessert. It didn't seem to disturb Rhodes at all that the railway and the road to Simonstown ran between him and the beach. Perhaps he knew he neared the end of the journey and had resigned himself to it. He often repeated the same phrase: "So much to do, so little time to do it." Catherine Radziwill launched into one of her interminable Russian reminiscences, inspired by the menu on her plate.

"In Saint Petersburg at the Pjatino Palace they served us peewit eggs for breakfast," she informed them. "The servants went out every night searching the flats along the Neva. We would watch their lanterns reflected in the marshes." She sighed romantically. She meant to make it clear to the two men that she possessed a dazzling past beyond their wildest dreams. This tragic-comic state of affairs often struck her as a perverse joke: a princess who had been at home in the Winter Palace, who had walked and talked with Tsars and Emperors, sitting in a rabbit hutch by a railway line!

Jameson remained unimpressed. He played nonchalantly with the stem of his wine glass.

"But I always thought, Princess, that you were Polish by birth," he remarked, seeking the weak link in her armor. A spot of color rose to Catherine's pale cheek.

"My father had no love for the Polish cause," she insisted on the defensive. "He was essentially a Russian in opinions, ideas and affections. He loved Russia with a passionate devotion, like I do."

"I wonder that you ever left then," retorted the doctor with a sweet smile. A little yelp of contrived laughter escaped Catherine's lips and trailed off into an embarrassed silence. She hated Jameson. She loathed him because he could see through her façade. He knew too much about her past and her father's treacherous betrayal of his own people. He had checked up on the trail of scandal that had followed her across Eastern Europe. It had finally driven her to seek asylum in the relative obscurity of the African continent. She hated him most because he loved Rhodes, which made him her rival.

"Dear me!" she exclaimed. "I do believe I've left my journal at the villa, and I did want to read you something very important." She turned to her host. Her once-sensual lips parted in a smile of complicity. Her dark gypsy eyes flashed at him like a beacon on a foggy night. "I'm sure the doctor wouldn't mind driving over and fetching it," she purred. "My maid will tell him where it is." Rhodes blushed and ran a hand through his tousled hair.

"Yes, do be a good fellow, Jameson and... and.." The doctor struggled to his feet with a groan. His flushed face showed clearly that he considered his friend the most absurdly feeble person alive. He behaved roughly, even brutally, with men, but with a woman... bah! Enough to make one sick! He shrugged his shoulders and slipped off the verandah. The gate at the end of the dusty yard creaked.

Even before Jameson's footsteps on the road had died away, Catherine was on her feet. She flitted round the table and sat in the chair next to Rhodes. Her hand with rings on almost every finger reached out for his. Then she thought better of the move and the hand dropped back onto her lap. She laughed breathlessly.

"To anyone but you," she began, biting her lower lip, "these words would be impossible to pronounce, but allow me to say that in the bitterness of being for the first time in my life obliged to ask anybody for help, I put my pride aside and tell you quite frankly that you are the only person from whom I should accept anything. I do so with gratitude." Rhodes failed to react. A group of noisy children passed along the road, rolling wooden hoops in the dust and screaming with excitement. In the scrubland behind the shack, the shrill rattle of a shrike broke the silence then subsided to a subdued monotonous warble. The princess tried to assemble her wits. She needed money. What story could she invent before Jameson returned? She could lay the blame on her son; say that the boy had been so ashamed of his mother having to work for a living that he had gambled on the stock market and lost money that she had been obliged to repay. Anything. Certainly things could not continue like this any longer. She didn't even have the money to pay her rent. She leaned confidently closer to Rhodes.

"Will you help me out of this muddle and give me, not your money, but your security for a year with the Standard Bank?" she asked. "Three thousand pounds should be enough. I shall return the money directly to the bank. It will enable me to live in peace and earn my daily bread. I can go to London for a month to see about the publication of my two books." Rhodes looked perplexed. It was the first time he'd heard anything about the princess being an author. He waited politely for confirmation. Catherine laughed again.

"Did I never lend you a copy of my book 'The Resurrection of Peter'?" she cried too boisterously. "How thoughtless of me!" In fact, the book in question, a reply to Olive Schreiner's attack on Rhodes, had not gone beyond manuscript form and remained totally unknown to the publishing world. Still Rhodes said nothing. Catherine clutched at a second straw.

"I have been offered the correspondentship of 'The Morning Post' and the 'Daily Mail', at the rate of £250 a year for each paper. I also receive an annual income of £1500 from my divorce." Two more lies! Both newspapers had excellent correspondents in South Africa and many years would pass before she finally got a divorce from Wilhelm Radziwill. She began to panic. Rhodes tapped nervously on the table with his strong miner's fingers. The purple tinge in his puffy face deepened. Catherine's assumption that she could gull him that easily angered him. He had a violent temper. He would have to keep it in check. He knew from a mutual friend, Dr. Schultz, that the Princess had been unable to pay her bills at the Mount Nelson Hotel. Certainly the rent on her Muizeberg villa hadn't been met. He knew that the papers she mentioned offered her nothing in the way of employment. It was all lies from beginning to end! Slowly he rose to his feet. He felt tired and his doctors had warned him about his heart condition. Catherine laid a hand on his arm to stop him.

"Later on I shall go up to Johannesburg and Kimberly with my boy," she explained. "If I had the sum I mentioned, I would get through quietly and no longer live in dread of the next day. I would return the money in a year. Will you give me this security?" Rhodes blinked.

"Excuse me a minute," he muttered, went to the sideboard and poured himself a whiskey. With the glass in his hand, he lumbered into the next room, used as a temporary office. Phillip Jourdain sat at the desk bent over a pile of papers.

"May I get you anything, sir?" Rhodes shook his head impatiently.

"Instruct Syfret to look into the Princess's financial state," he ordered. "He will propose to her that if she leaves the country and returns to Europe, I shall settle all her bills for her." He took his battered felt hat from the peg in the hall and crept cautiously out of the cottage by the back door without a glance at the verandah. He mounted his horse and rode through the scattered rocks and violet flowering sage. The powerful aroma of the crushed shrubs under his horse's hoofs made him sigh with sensual pleasure. For centuries the woody-based sage plant had been used to cleanse habitations. A pity it couldn't cleanse him of the Princess's presence!

Ten minutes after his departure Dr. Jameson returned. He had failed to find the missing journal, which had never left

Catherine Radziwill's handbag. He met her standing on the steps.

"What can one do with Mr. Rhodes?" she exclaimed with an uneasy laugh. "He has simply disappeared."

"Leave him alone," replied the doctor and strode past her into the cottage. The Princess only met with Rhodes one more time, when she asked him to marry her. He refused and she sought revenge by forging his signature on a promissory note. The court finally condemned her to four months in prison after weeks of a scandalous trial.

Louise Juta watched the Princess walking slowly down the dusty lane under her extravagantly elaborate parasol. Tired of exploring the familiar rock pools below the house with her brother, Louise had wandered into the chaotic wilderness of weathered sandstone blocks that bordered Kalk Bay in search of chameleons. To the seven-year old girl the capacity of these creatures to change their color to match the background was a source of both mystery and marvel. Mr. Sclater at the museum had gone to some trouble to satisfy her curiosity. He pointed out that their bizarre appearance stemmed from the large eyes and fused eyelids. Independently moveable, they swiveled into position when a prey was located. Louise had sometimes stayed immobile for fifteen minutes or more among the rocks watching a chameleon stalking a beetle. Once within range, the sticky-tipped tongue shot out and retracted rapidly with the victim securely stuck to it. Sometimes she might stumble on a clutch of forty eggs in the earth or under a rotting log, although most of the South African chameleons bore their young alive.

Jan had remained among the rock pools, wading in the flower gardens of sea anemones and scarlet star fish. The rest of the family had retired to their shuttered bedrooms, where the ceiling fans purred peacefully and rocked them into the drowsy somnolence of early afternoon siesta. Plunged into silent shadiness, the beach house seemed almost moribund to Louise. So much waited to be explored and discovered outside in the sunshine. She watched the Princess's parasol pass under the tamarisk trees. It made her remember the time Amar, their Malay laundress, had been allowed to take her to the marriage ceremony of someone in her family. All the guests carried parasols, even when they danced. Then the young couple walked slowly three times round a fire, and took seven steps backwards with their garments knotted together. The bride's father led them to a bed, surrounded by richly decorated drapes, built high up near the ceiling in the bridal bedroom. The couple climbed the ladder and drew the curtains behind them. Outside the dance continued. After the visit Louise had reported to Jan.

"Amar said that the girl had to cry for three days before the wedding or her parents beat her," she informed him on arrival home from the ceremony. Jan wasn't listening. He had caught sight of eight chacma baboons converging on 'Mon Desir'. With much grunting and squealing, the closely-knit group swarmed through the surrounding thorn scrub under the leadership of a powerful male. His coarse coat of matted hair hung over his shoulders like cape. The tribe paused at the boundary fence. Their bulging cheek pouches and long truncated muzzles quivered in anticipation of a potential feast. With a bark and a series of chattered signals, the leader arched his tail and led his harem into the kitchen garden and among the water melons. A mixture of fear and fascination prevented the two children from intervening. Baboons belonged to the mysterious realm of twilight mountain slopes and misty shadows. Baboons seldom approached human habitations. When they did, Man had every cause for alarm. Henry Juta had often warned his family to be cautious in their presence.

"Because of their enormous canines and powerful limbs," he cautioned them, "baboons can be very destructive to crops and dangerous adversaries. Moreover, they are inveterate thieves with a very definite means of communication. They use their tails to signal." Jan and Louise stood like statues watching the animals rip into the melons, nostrils quivering, naked buttocks an almost obscene vermilion in the late afternoon light. They remembered a story that Marley, the cook, had brought back from the coast a few weeks before. A fisherman at Witsandbaai had left his three month-old baby girl lying in the sun at the back of the hut, while he went down to the beach to load his nets in the boat. On his return the baby had disappeared. He first thought that his wife had come home and taken the baby inside. After several hours of frantic searching, involving the whole village, they found the baby on the upper slopes of the Flatkop, over a thousand feet above sea level in the vicinity of a baboon colony. She was miraculously unharmed but very hungry. Her cries had probably put the baboons to flight. A young baboon never cries. Louise felt comforted by the thought that she was far too chubby for even the biggest baboon to carry off.

"They'd never get you farther than ten yards," jeered Jan, sensing his sister's uneasiness. She had inherited the heavy bone structure of her Dutch and German ancestors. In the pseudo-aristocratic circles her family moved through, a certain 'rondeur' indicated a healthy constitution.

The back door opened with a crash. The huge male sprang away with a startled bark, followed by his chattering troop. Marley appeared on the threshold like a god in a roadside shrine, waving an enormous soup ladle. The marauding baboons had reduced the melon patch to a trampled mess of melon rind and scattered seeds. Jan galloped down the lawn and into the house. Louise wandered to the old tree house. The remembered story of the baby and the baboons had stirred deeper thoughts, pricked a hidden consciousness as to the importance of life itself. Was she really little more than a plump ball of puppy fat in a sailor suit? What lay beneath? Beneath what she seemed to be or was supposed to be or what her parents had called her. Perhaps the source of her restlessness resided in her name. Yes, that's what it was! With a sudden sense of relief, she rushed to the fishing-room, where her father prepared his tackle.

"Papie! Why did you give me such awful names?" she demanded. "I hate them! They're not me at all! You should have treated me like those ancient Egyptians you're always telling us about. Parents never gave their children names until they saw what kind of character they had." Henry Juta nodded and stroked his clean-shaven chin. He finished winding in the fishing reel and leant the long supple rod against the wall.

"I must see what can be done. You'll be nine in a few days. Perhaps before then I'll think of a new name for you." He turned his attention to the wooden board screwed to the wall, where an array of hooks hung in orderly rows.

The birthday morning dawned. On her way to breakfast Louise met her father coming out of his study. He called her in.

"Well, child," he announced. "I think I have a name for you, It isn't really a name at all. It's a sound. You have a great gift that has already proved itself—an unusual voice. You appreciate the sounds of nature better than any of us. You will hear them in this word. So here it is, your new name: 'Luia'." Louise closed her eyes. Luia! What could she hear in it? The muffled boom of Atlantic breakers on a sand-besieged shore? The dry scratch of lizard claws on a sandstone shelf? The west wind whispering through swaying pines? Loud bugle-calling web-footed gray and black gulls soaring above fishing boats? The stealthy rustle of a snake in the lake-side lilies? Bursts of meaning in a child's world of inevitable confusion.

"It's a lovely name, Papie," she said at last. "And it's me. I know it is!" Her chubby face held an expression of enchanted gravity as she kissed her father on the cheek. That evening she was allowed to stay up in her tree house longer than usual. Among the sweet-scented acacias the persistent rattle of the cicadas faded into silence. The dusk-troubled lions in their enclosure at Rondebosch coughed a salute to the rising moon. Luia climbed down in the deepening dark and ran into the house.

In October the storm that had been menacing the country for so long burst. Imperial troops moved north to Kimberley and Mafeking. British reinforcements poured into Natal from India. They landed at Durban on the Pacific coast. Originally named Port Natal by Vasco da Gama because he sighted it on Christmas Day 1497, the British later settled on a strip of coast ceded by the Zulu despot Chaka. They progressively consolidated the outpost and the white population had reached thirty-five by 1835.

In the Transvaal Kruger called out the burgher militia and everyone waited for something to happen. The Juta children hardly noticed the tension in the air. Cape Town lay far to the south of the Transvaal border. Life in the little 'museum' continued as always. Jan concentrated on pinning up two new butterflies. At the other end of the wooden shed Luia bent over the latest batch of pot sherds from Mr. Sclater, painstakingly labeling each fragment. On the main lawn Henry Juta and William Schreiner sat at the tea table with Grandmother Henrietta Tait. Under the pergola Brenda and Renée, home for the long summer holiday, entertained two young Naval officers. At sixteen Renée aroused considerable interest among the naval officers stationed at Simonstown. After being screened by the parents, they appeared every Tuesday and Thursday afternoon like bees round a honey jar. Helen Juta had gone to town to chair a meeting of the Needlework Guild, which she had founded on the model of Lady Wolverton's success in England. No threat of war six hundred miles to the north disturbed the cosy security of Cape Town social activities.

The distant thrill of a bugle call floated through the pines from the direction of Wynberg Barracks. Luia looked up from the broken pots. Four o'clock. That meant Grandmother Henrietta would shortly come cane-tapping along the flagged path to pay them a visit. She glanced apprehensively through the trees. The sinking sun reverberated obliquely off the whitewashed walls of the house. It accentuated the contrast made by the dark teak shutters and the slates on the roof. In the shade of the library verandah a uniformed servant rearranged the wicker chairs. Luia abandoned her pottery and reached for a large square biscuit tin with a perforated lid.

Something moved inside. Cautiously Luia removed the lid and lifted out a vivid green chameleon, the latest addition to the Luia Juta Natural Science Laboratory. She dropped the unfortunate reptile onto a square of red cloth. The scaly head jerked from side to side, the independent eyes swiveling at all angles in perplexity. The creature's attempt to assume the new color only resulted in a dark green ground spotted with reddish patches. Luia looked over at her brother.

"Why do you think they change color?" she asked. Her tone of voice suggested that she expected him to give the wrong answer.

"Camouflage, of course!" Jan retorted at once, concentrating on a minute study of a butterfly's head through his magnifying glass. Luia snorted and shook her head vigorously. She tried to remember what she had read about it; something to do with the light or the temperature. Anyway it wasn't to camouflage themselves as Jan thought. He brushed a lock of blond hair off his forehead.

"What is it then, clever?" Luia pretended to think profoundly.

"The light," she said a little lamely and hastily changed the subject. "Let's watch them feed." She lifted another two lizards from the tin. In the humid heat of the little hut flies buzzed with indefatigable insistence against the dusty window pane and the ubiquitous pot of flowers. This love of flowering plants formed a part of the reason her austere maternal grandmother came so often to visit the children. The irascible short-tempered old lady, who made her aristocratic ancestry apparent in all her movements, knew more about the local flora than most people born in the Cape. Every Saturday afternoon brought a new lesson on some aspect of horticulture. Perhaps it was the only way she knew how to express her love, to enlighten with her knowledge those she loved. But Luia would always retain an discomforting childhood image, a haunting amalgamation of the Red Queen from 'Alice in Wonderland', ordering the gardeners to have their heads chopped off and the blind beggar pirate in 'Treasure Island' tapping his stick along the road to the Benbow Inn.

One of the chameleons soon set its sights on a trapped fly. It stalked it with almost insolent nonchalance. Then its long tubular tongue shot out with lightning speed and telescoped back round the slippery spike of bone in its mouth with the fly securely stuck to the tip.

The tapping stick approached along the paving stones in the pine wood. Back straight as a ramrod, Grandmother Henrietta advanced inexorably towards her goal. In her imposing wake walked her son-in-law with a round wicker basket containing a pair of secateurs and thick gardening gloves.

"I bet you she won't come in," whispered Jan, spying on the strolling couple through a knot hole. "When she wants to cut roses, she never comes in, but let's get out before they arrive, just the same." Too late! They bumped into the old lady before they could slip round the corner.

"There you are! Where have you been hiding? In that horrible tree again, I suppose!" Athough perfectly aware that the children had just come out of the 'museum', Grandmother Tait never lost an opportunity of attacking her son-in-law for his allowing Luia to indulge in her tree-climbing passion. "I can't think why you allow your daughter to swing about in trees like a monkey, Juta!" This verbal castigation left Henry Juta impassive. He had heard it too many times. He took Luia's hand.

"Oh, I don't think it does her any harm, Mrs. Tait." This was the conventional reply to the conventional censure. They waited for the conventional conclusion. The cantankerous harridan raised her eyebrows.

"We're all entitled to opinions, Juta. Unfortunately! Well, come along!" The procession progressed to the rose garden, where they penetrated a world of orderly perfection. Beyond a dense shrubbery of white and yellow gardenias interspersed with evergreen camellia bushes, lay long beds of many-colored roses. In a large oval central bed blossomed dozens of pink rose bushes. Passion flowers and deep blue

clematis twined round a trellised pergola at the far end, con-
cealing the kitchen garden. Grandmother Henrietta halted
in front of a recently-planted group of Orleans roses. She
turned on Luia.

"What conditions are essential to a rose, child?" she demanded. Luia had little difficulty with that. She had been
asked the same question more than a dozen times.

"A full sun, good drainage and thorough watering, and
they shouldn't be planted too close to other plants, particularly trees," she recited, straight from the horse's mouth. She
looked to her father for approval. Henry Juta, however, had
spotted a dead branch on one of his prized gardenia bushes
and hurried over to repair the disgrace. With her cane, Grandmother Henrietta prodded the soil at the base of a magnifi-
cent yellow hybrid.

"And why do we mould the soil around the base?" Luia
hesitated.

"I suppose it's to stop the stem from drying out," she replied. She stared at the little mound of compost as if she
hoped to see the answer written there. The old lady snorted.

"You shouldn't suppose, you should know!" she snapped.
Like a general on troop inspection, she led the way to the
next station, a deep red rose that Luia had recently grafted
under her grandmother's eagle eye. She stooped, pushed her
gold-rimmed spectacles to the end of her nose, and inspected
the results. "Your child's work, Juta" she admitted almost reluctantly. "Without any help from me." With a sudden shrug
of the shoulders, she straightened her back and vanished
round the side of the house to inspect Helen Juta's collection
of exotic ferns.

Jan and Luia scampered back to the 'museum' to complete the afternoon's tasks. Their father strolled thoughtfully
across the gravel drive to the main lawn. Schreiner sat at
the massive teak garden table alone. The three older girls
had gone to play tennis with the naval officers. Their excited
voices rose sporadically from the court beyond the shrubbery. Henry Juta almost wished they had stayed a bit longer

at the tea table. Being alone with the depressed Prime Minister brought the unpleasant reality home too vividly. Schreiner read his thoughts.

"Well, Buddie, the storm has burst," he muttered despondently. He had driven Rhodes out of power to save the country and now the country faced certain war with the Boers. Perhaps things would have been better if Rhodes had stayed in power. He realized, however, that Britain needed a scapegoat and he fitted the bill far better than the dominating megalomaniac millionaire. He rubbed his eyes and groaned. "All that one can do now is try and guide the helm of the Colony so that it may not make shipwreck," he grumbled. "Thank God a man may yet serve loyally both dear old England and the South Africa that is even dearer to her sons." He thought of his own sons. They would still not speak to him because of his split with Rhodes. Henry Juta contemplated his harassed friend sadly. The good old college days in England seemed incredibly remote, drifting in the un-dreamed of realm of future fame and formidable responsibility. The perfect precision of the law they had once admired so much no longer had an adequate answer to give. Henry Juta patted him on the shoulder.

"It will be a short war. You'll see," he forecast, but the words sounded hollow, based more on hope than on faith. The muffled thunder of artillery from the Wynberg Barracks, already on full alert, rolled round the mountain. The gunners practiced by shelling the cliffs under Devil's Peak. The sound of impacted shells had become as common as the cooing doves on the roof.

"How's Olive?" asked Henry Juta casually. Schreiner smiled wanly.

"Curiously enough my little sister is still making excuses for the Imperial government on one hand while attacking it with all the weapons she can muster on the other. Nevertheless..." he faltered. His friend knew why. Since the prospect of war had become a reality, Olive had returned from Johannesburg with her husband and moved in with Schreiner. Her ferocious support for the Boers embarrassed the Prime Minister, whose whole policy aimed at appeasement.

The sound of a horse cantering up the gravel drive disrupted their conversation. A youthful subaltern appeared through the swaying pines. He dismounted in front of the stoep and crossed the lawn. Saluting the Prime Minister, he handed him a sealed dispatch. His arrival had been observed from the tennis court. The five young people came anxiously down the flagged path still clutching their rackets. A few whispered words brought the officers to attention.

"I'm afraid we must get away at once," the elder officer said. "So sorry to have to leave you in this way." He sounded sorry too as he looked at the flushed girls, hair coming loose, adolescent bosoms heaving.

"Forgive us, my dears, will you?" his partner pleaded, knowing full well that it might be some time before they set foot in the Juta home again. To Renée they suddenly looked very young and vulnerable. They made her feel almost maternal. In a few weeks those beautiful Adonis bodies might lie mutilated on the battlefield, not killed heroically by a boar but by a stray Boer shell. The mask of masculine assurance had slipped awry.

"It can't be war!" she gasped. "How fightful! Must you go?" Already a servant had been summoned to bring the horses round to the front from the stables. Schreiner raised his eyes from the dispatch.

"Well, gentlemen." He announced. "General Joubert has moved south from Pretoria and surrounded Kimberley." He knew why. The Boers wanted to capture Rhodes and 'exhibit him in a cage', as Kruger put it. Rhodes! Always Rhodes! The Transvaal army's mission was not to capture the Cape Constabulary or a British regiment but just one man. It might almost have been funny. Rhodes had insisted on going back to Kimberley, where he had first founded his empire, despite repeated warnings from his friends. Even the mayor of Kimberley had suggested diplomatically that he postpone his visit, but Rhodes' mind turned resolutely round the cradle of his fortune, the De Beers Consolidated Mines, still the source of his immense income. Founded in 1888 with funding by the Rothschild family, Rhodes' company soon controlled all the mining operations in the country. Now the Boers had cooped him up amid his marvelous mines. Hard luck! Let them put Rhodes in a cage and see if William Schreiner lost any sleep over it.

The three horses cantered through the trees. The girls waved. From the nursery window Luia watched the flashing figures in their scarlet uniforms reach the end of the drive and turn into Main Road. She only saw the glamour and the heroics of the war that was about to begin, where fine ladies like her mother played Florence Nightingale and so many of the handsome young officers never returned.

6

Kimberley House shimmered behind a shroud of pulsating dust at the far end of Du Toitspan Road. Behind closed doors, the habitual hum of diamond brokers had ceased, a mere memory of a bygone golden age. Beyond the illusive line of picket fences that marked the town perimeter lay the Boer encampment and the purple hills of the Orange Free State. At the beginning of the century, trekboers, nomadic pastoral farmers, ever looking for new pastures and land to farm, began seasonal grazing across the Orange River. In 1835 The Great Trek resulted in the exodus of two thousand frontier folk, mainly Boers, pushed north by resentment against British colonial policy in the Cape. The trekkers mapped out and planned a republic. The Jameson Raid had inflamed public opinion. Free State commandos manned the frontier. A wave of pro-Transvaal sentiment swept the republic. President Steyn, however, continued to counsel moderation. He urged the Transvaal president Kruger to accept any compromise that would avert war, but refused to accept the British offer of neutrality. For eighty-two days his commandos had surrounded Kimberley, the sacred seat of the diamond kings, situated just outside the Free State border.

In the besieged town, Colonel Kekewick had set up his headquarters on the first floor of an office building in Stockdale Street. From his window he looked across at the Consolidated Building, home of Rhodes' De Beers Consolidated Mines. From this central position he had one foot in the sacred cell of the queen bee. Nothing of note could happen without Colonel Kekewick seeing it. Unfortunately, Rhodes had failed to escape before the Boer scouts had cut the railway line to the south. Founded only twenty-five years before by diggers who discovered diamonds on the farms, the inhabitants of Kimberley now faced starvation and daily shelling.

Colonel Kekewick paced to and fro above the deserted street. A fickle wind off the veldt chased yellowed newspapers along the hastily-improvised wooden pavements. The troops had erected scaffolding against the facades of many houses to support the extra weight of sandbags piled along first floor balconies. The colonel moved the lace curtain a few inches. At the far end of the bare dusty street a small procession had turned in from Market Square. At its head rode Cecil Rhodes, heavy, bovine and visibly in poor health, dressed in the familiar white flannel trousers, brown tweed coat and narrow-brimmed felt hat. Faces appeared at windows. People applauded from balconies and stable doors. Kekewick swore and turned to his ADC.

"He's been warned not to make himself so conspicuous," he grumbled. "Anyone can see him a mile away. There's nothing the Boers would like better than to knock him off that horse!" It annoyed him that he had to admit to a certain jealous admiration for the statesman, capable of rousing so much enthusiasm just by appearing on the street. Outside the telegraph office Rhodes stopped to chat with a group of mounted militia. They touched their peaked caps respectfully and then cantered off in the direction of Kenilworth. The colonel rubbed the side of his nose.

"Any idea what he's up to out there?" he wondered. The captain looked up from his paper work.

"Mr. Rhodes, sir?"

"Yes. Why is he so interested in Kenilworth? That's the fifth day running he's sent men out there."

"I gather they're building a fort, sir." The captain tried to keep his voice as neutral as possible. Kekewick exploded.

"A fort! You mean to tell me that Mr. Rhodes is building a fort at Kenilworth? What on earth for?"

"I gather it's to house the cavalry unit he mustered last week, sir." The captain stared at his boots.

"You gather! You gather! Why wasn't I informed of this?" A fly landed on his whiskered cheek. Kekewick lunged at it. With a muffled drone the damaged insect spiraled away on one wing. The colonel slumped into his chair and mopped his brow.

"A fort at Kenilworth. It's quite unnecessary. Totally unnecessary!" he growled. It was the last straw. He had tolerated Rhodes' soup kitchens, his coal dumps, his search lights and barrage balloons, his shell-proof shelters and the ten thousand natives he had enlisted to build roads inside the town perimeter. He had even turned a blind eye to the formation of an eight hundred man cavalry unit, but a fort....! He thumped the table.

"Captain! Send for Mr. Jourdain. At once!" With the captain out of the room he shrugged his shoulders and sighed. He knew that with or without his permission Rhodes would continue to do what he pleased. Rhodes and his millions was Kimberley. Kekewick was military commander in name only. In reality he commanded nothing.

In the street Rhodes' cavalcade had stopped again. Visibly critical, Rhodes observed a work shift digging a trench across the street from the central Post Office. Every few minutes the ground shook to the thud of distant artillery. No one paid the slightest attention. Rhodes engaged a conversation with the wife of one of his mine directors.

"My dear Julia," he protested. "Everyone asks me why I don't get married. I cannot get married. I have too much work on my hands. I should always be away from home and quite unable to do my duty as a loving husband. A married man should be at home to give the attention and advice that a wife expects from her husband." Anyway, he thought, you could never trust a woman. What woman had ever brought him a second's real pleasure? They had all proved scheming and malicious like Olive Schreiner and Princess Radziwill.

The only woman whose company he appreciated was Mrs. Koopmans de Wet, and she was eighty-five!

He noticed something about the trench that didn't suit him. Having ascertained from the duty sergeant that Colonel Kekewick himself had given the order, he grunted and waved a disdainful hand in the air.

"The man doesn't know his job," he muttered. A shell burst behind the Law Court. Glass shattered and a woman screamed. Rhodes ignored it. More and more his thoughts turned to Kimberley in the old days, just a collection of simple farms and three competing diamond camps. True friendships had been founded there: Neville Pickering, who had died in a riding accident; Starr Jameson, still severely ill after his prison sentence and ruining his friend's political career; Barney Barnato, one of the most colorful characters in the early Kimberley. Born in London of Jewish parents he had been a prizefighter and music-hall turn before joining his brother in the diamond mines. He had arrived from the London slums with sixty boxes of dubious cigars and become as rich as Rhodes himself. Suffering from depression after Jameson's abortive raid, Barney had mysteriously disappeared overboard off the island of Madeira three years ago on the way back to England. In those distant days British and Dutch had dug together in harmony too. None of today's nationalistic antagonism.

"In spite of it all, I like the Dutch," he remarked to Julia Maguire as another shell crashed somewhere near the railway station. "I like their courtesy, their homely tenacity of purpose. We always used to get along well together, but now they've made me the most abused man in Africa." He sounded so sorry for himself that Julia Maguire smiled. She had known Rhodes a long time too. Her Irish husband had studied law at Oxford with him. He had perfidiously negotiated with the last Matabele chief, Lobengula, on behalf of the Chartered Company. Lobengula had also died mysteriously, some said of smallpox, others dysentery and poison had been mentioned. The British Crown had taken his county and Matabeleland had become Rhodesia. The elegant Rochfort Maguire, often caricatured in 'Vanity Fair', wielded more power and influence than any of Rhodes' associates. He continued in his role as director of Consolidated Gold Fields and the Rhodesian Railway until his death more than twenty years later. The statesman caught Julia Maguire's smile and chuckled.

"Now they've made it my duty to stand up on behalf of the rights of the pastoral Dutch against the overbearing domination of our own people," he objected cynically. The familiar whine of self-pity crept into his high-pitched voice. "Still, if Oom Paul has any sense, he'll climb down in the end and there'll be a settlement." Unfortunately, the fanatically religious Paul Kruger had decided that God's word should be his rule of conduct in politics and the foundation upon which the Transvaal had to be established. He would lose his country, escape to Europe and die in exile in Switzerland four years later.

Rhodes caught sight of Colonel Kekewick's ADC walking towards them purposefully and broke into a broad boyish grin. He turned to his secretary.

"Quick, Jourdain! Into the Post Office. I've just remembered I have to telegraph Baden-Powell and find out what's happening in Mafeking." Before the captain could reach Rhodes, he had slipped into the Post Office, shut himself into the small room at the back and given the postmaster orders not to disturb him. Like a mischievous schoolboy playing a prank on the teacher, he glued his ear to the door. He heard the captain arguing with the postmaster and getting nowhere. After five minutes the sound of his cavalry boots clattered over the creaking wooden floor and faded into the distance. Rhodes shook his head sadly.

"The man doesn't know his job! A soldier! It's simply a matter of common sense". He plopped heavily into an armchair and mopped his sweating brow. The inherited tuberculosis had once been a worry, now it was his heart. No doubt it was all imagination, but it seemed that lately he experienced pains in the chest that radiated to his neck, sometimes even his teeth, whenever he got excited. Perhaps knowing that he had not much longer to live, he had recently written his will, for the fifth time. In it he expressed the wish that one day a power might be founded, great enough to make war impossible. Life had become a mosaic of memories: dusks on the stoep at Groote Schuur, the peaceful plod of hoofs under Table Mountain, pork chops on the veldt with Grimmer, Colesberg Kopje swarming with ten thousand diggers or farther back still those solitary walks in the woods around Bishop's Storton.

Philip Jourdain stood quietly by the door. He had noticed his employer's increasing obsession with death and the shortness of life. He had once overheard a conversation between Rhodes and Jameson. Rhodes had looked puffier than usual, the veins on his face swollen, his brow wet with sweat.

"At any rate, Jameson," he argued, "death from the heart is clean and quick. There's nothing repulsive or lingering about it. It is a clean death, isn't it?" Jourdain hadn't heard the doctor's reply. He had probably fobbed it off with a typical pleasantry. He realized that Rhodes was talking to him, hunched up in his chair with a hand to his chest.

"The great fault in life, Philip," he said, "is its shortness, its fragility, its ephemeral quality. Like friendships betrayed," he added: another of the burdens he had to bear! How many of the men to whom he had offered friendship had remained true? Neville Pickering had died. Harry Currey had got engaged and left his service. Jameson had ruined his career. Had he anything to expect from this new friendship with Rudyard Kipling? He tried to recall what he had heard about the famous writer and his wife. When Carrie Balestier had met Kipling he was twenty-four and she four years his senior and rather plain. She had come to London with her brother Walcott, looking for English authors interested in the prospect of secure American sales. Rumors circulated that it was not Carrie with whom Kipling fell in love, but her brother. When Walcott died of typhoid fever in Germany, Kipling proposed marriage and was accepted by Carrie. His family and most of his literary friends took against her, describing her as 'a hard little person'. Married life started badly when they visited Carrie's family in Vermont and briefly lived there, until Carrie quarreled with her family about property and they returned to England. Kipling's own family never forgave her, considering her an adventuress. When Josephine, their eldest daughter, died, a pall settled over their gloomy liaison, but Carrie continued her capable services to her husband and his work, overseeing his life and leaving him a martyr to severe stomach pains.

Rhodes had made the opening move by offering the Kiplings his cottage, 'The Woolsack,' at Bishop's Lea. A miniature replica of a Dutch house, with white pillars and slate roof it had been designed by Herbert Baker, the architect who had renovated Groote Schuur and built the Juta home. The damp windy winters in England had driven Kipling and his family to the milder South Seas until the spring. He now had a home to go to and a man after his own heart waiting to welcome him each year. Rhodes pictured them strolling together through the blazing hydrangea fields or on the stoep sipping his favorite Nyasaland coffee. Kipling would become the receptive ear for new ideas and plans. They had to discuss his project for the scholarships. He would send bright young men to Oxford to promote an attachment to their new country, but without withdrawing them or their sympathies from the land of their birth. The Rhodes Scholarships! His lips mouthed the words. Carving out a future for Africa and a glorious past for himself. He liked to recall Kipling's lines on the subject: 'Wherefore praise we famous men from whose bays we borrow? They that put aside Today, all the joys of their Today, and with the toil of their Today bought for us Tomorrow,'

Another Boer shell exploded at the end of the street. Shop windows rattled convulsively as though the frail plaster walls held imprisoned a poltergeist trying to get out. One or two panes of glass fell out onto the sidewalk. Rhodes held his hand to his heart and dreamed.

More than two hundred miles farther north on the banks of the muddy Molopo River the inhabitants of the recently-founded township of Mefeking gazed anxiously over the dry plain towards the Transvaal border, barely ten miles distant. Founded only fifteen years earlier as headquarters of the railway between Kimberley and Bulawayo, the town had been surrounded by six thousand Boers since October. To the British commander, Colonel Robert Baden-Powell, the enemy's failure to attack him remained a mystery. Only one feeble assault had been attempted on Cannon Kopje, repulsed with heavy losses on both sides. Since the outbreak of war other British townships had fallen : Stormberg, Maggersfontein and Colenso, Kimberley and Ladysmith besieged, but the six thousand Boers outside Mafeking simply sat in the bush and sniped ineffectually at the perimeter defenses. Nominal command of Boer operations was assumed by General Piet Joubert. A direct descendant of French Hugenots who fled to South Africa in 1688 after the revocation of the Edict of Nantes, Joubert's position had become weakened by accusations of treachery and of sympathy with the Uitlander agitation. He lacked determination and assertiveness and acted mainly on the defensive. A year later he would die from peritonitis, 'a soldier and a gentleman and a brave and honorable opponent'.

In his improvised HQ behind the railway workshops Baden-Powell brought the morning's briefing to an end. Each day he met with his senior officers to discuss information gleaned from the previous night's espionage excursions behind the Boer lines. A mass of useful data had been accumulated with which to counteract any future enemy aggression. The colonel loved the night. He personally joined scouting missions into the veldt, then back on his camp mattress on the verandah, he would lie awake, tracing in his mind the various stratagems by which he could forestall an enemy five times superior. He encouraged personal initiative in his troops, even at the risk of making a mistake. He had been accused four years earlier of illegally executing a prisoner of war, Matabele chief Uwini, who had been promised his life would be spared if he surrendered.

"A man who never made a mistake never made anything," he told them. "Not that I'm suggesting that you should get into the habit of making mistakes, gentlemen," he added, rolling up the maps they had been studying. Slim and graceful in his neat brown uniform and wide-brimmed felt bush hat, he inspired admiration and affection among his motley force of miscellaneous units, including two hundred cadets of between twelve and fifteen years old. Baden-Powell used them to stand guard, carry messages and assist in the hospital. These boys impressed him and he later used their courage as an object lesson in his book 'Scouting for Boys'.

The wooden walls and corrugated tin roof of the workshop rattled as another shell exploded. Since the opening of the siege seven months before, more than twenty thousand shells had landed in the town, a sinister syncopation underlying the more bucolic sounds of the journeying winds, the warm and gentle veldt breezes, redolent with the weedy fragrance of the Molopo River.

Baden-Powell smoothed his bushy walrus mustache and straightened the lapel of his uniform.

"There you have it, gentlemen," he concluded. "Bluff the enemy with a show of force you don't have. The more the better. But don't let yourself get out of touch with your own side without orders. You may draw them into difficulties in their endeavor to support you. That's all." He watched his group leaders file out into heat-hazed afternoon sunlight. He rubbed his eyes at the glare beyond the workshop roof. Psychedelic shapes danced on the floor at his feet. He pursed his lips. He had fewer than a thousand trained troops with which to hold off General Cronje, and half of them were equipped with obsolete Martini-Henry single loaders. He turned to Major Panzera, his liaison officer.

"What's the report on the Hotchkiss?"

"Pretty hopeless, sir. Worn fittings, the carriage in disrepair and the fuses so shrunken with age that we'd have to wedge them into the shells with paper." Baden-Powell grunted, but no sign of disappointment or discouragement betrayed the mask of self-control that ruled his life. He began to whistle his favorite air from 'Cavalleria Rusticana'. Reaching for his swagger stick, he strode off to inspect the laying of a new series of home-made mines along the south perimeter. At the foot of Cannon Kopje, a hundred yards beyond the river, a column of natives transported the explosives from town in small boxes assembled by a mining expert. Carefully buried at fixed intervals around the perimeter, a maze of wires linked them to a central observation post. Panzera returned from a tour of inspection.

"Should be ready for action by six o'clock, sir," he reported. Baden-Powell glanced at his watch and climbed the ladder to the platform on top of the observation tower. In the haze, the township appeared as a vaguely colorful blot on the uniform drabness of the parched veldt. He swept the shimmering horizon with his field glasses. Clusters of Boer militia stood around idly at the foot of hastily-erected defenses. They wore no distinguishing uniform, unlike his own officers, some of whom still insisted on donning the brilliant scarlet jackets of their regiment, making them sitting targets on the colorless plain. As the colonel watched the Boers stepping warily over the coils of barbed wire that surrounded their outposts, an idea came to him. Distance and the African heat made it impossible to actually see the wire. You assumed its presence from the lines of posts driven in the earth and from the precautionary behavior of the men. Mafeking possessed no barbed wire. Why should that stop him from inventing imaginary wire defenses? He called down to Major Panzera.

"Didn't I see a whole stack of wooden poles down at the railway workshops?" he quizzed.

"Yes, sir. Telegraph poles."

"Good. Get a squad of men to cut them up into five-foot lengths and bring them over here tomorrow morning. Drive them into the ground all over the place. A forest of them. I'll brief the men afterwards." He turned his attention back to the dusk-darkening veldt and whistled softly to himself. In a few hours the Boers would be watching his men stepping out to stretch their legs, lifting them with the greatest care over coils of imaginary barbed wire. The power of assumption could be impressively strong.

As suddenly as he had appeared on the watch tower, Baden-Powell vanished to pay a call on Major Godley in charge of the western perimeter. The Major had recently remarked that one of the gate posts of a farm consisted of an old cannon. He had it dug up and it turned out to be an eighteenth century carronade. Coincidentally the cannon had 'B.P.& Co' engraved on the barrel. The resourceful mechanics at the workshops had made cannon balls to fit it and mounted it on a wooden carriage. For the past week it had competed with the Boer ninety-four pounder siege gun, known as 'Long Tom.'

Baden-Powell reached the firing area in time to witness a shot aimed down the main road to Johannesburg. With great interest all the men watched the flight of the projectile, which looked exactly like a dull gray cricket ball. It bumped down the road into the Boer laager among the wagons and tents, where one old Boer tried to field it. Immediately 'Long Tom' reposted. Everyone rushed for the extensive network of trenches and almost immediately rushed back to secure the trophy. Fifty percent of the Boer shells failed to burst. A soldier's active service record was based on the number of Boer shells he had in his possession. They acted as a currency of courage and also littered up the already congested barracks.

"Well bowled, Alex!" Baden-Powell picked up one of the hand-made missiles and turned it over in his hands. "Still, you might try and get some men out there tonight. See if they can get within range of 'Long Tom' and force them to shift her back a bit." The Boer accuracy had improved and not all the shells failed to explode. He slid down the side of a shallow pit in the sand. An extraordinary heap of miscellaneous metal junk sat under a low iron roof.

"Any luck last night?" the colonel asked an officer bent over the heap. This was 'The Wolf', Makeking's only howitzer, constructed out of the steam pipe of a railway engine with some iron railings melted down and shrunk into it. The whole astonishing contraption had been mounted on the wheels of an ancient threshing-machine. Baden-Powell recalled his description of 'The Wolf's' activities in his last letter home, smuggled out through the Boer lines at night.

"With home-made powder and shot, it doesn't carry very far. In order to make up for this, we have to move it out in the night as silently as we can, with the wheels wrapped up in canvas and straw, till we get within range of the Boer camp. Then we hang blankets all round the thing, so that the flash won't be visible and loose off shots as fast as we can. Then we lie low, while the Boers spend the rest of the night firing vaguely at where they think we are, which is generally where we aren't!"

Baden-Powell had never expected to see Africa again. His military career had send him all over the empire : Lucknow in 1877, the following year in Afghanistan, Zululand and his role in the operation to capture the Zulu chief Dinuzulu, Malta, Algeria, Ireland, the Gold Coast during the Ashanti War in 1895, back to South Africa for the Matabele War. When he had returned to England on the same boat as Rhodes in December 1896, he assumed that he had seen the last of the African continent. In reality he had first returned to India the following March. Then the rumors of war arrived from Cape Town and the entire regiment embarked for Durban. Baden-Powell, gazetted for 'extra regimental employ,' received three days warning in which to organize his departure. At his last interview with Field Marshal Viscount Garnet Wolseley, his old commander since the Ashanti days, he had anticipated the surprise. Wolseley judged a man's character by the way he reacted to surprises sprung on him. His own army career had begun during the Crimean War, where he had lost an eye at the siege of Sevastopol. He had distinguished himself at the relief of Lucknow, commanded the expedition to Ashanti and the expedition for the relief of General Gordon in Khartoum. Now he was responsible

for furnishing the unexpectedly large force required in South
Africa.

"I want you to go to South Africa", Wolseley said out of
the blue. "Can you go on Saturday next?"

"No, sir."

"Why not?" Baden-Powell had already checked on the
sailings of steamers to South Africa.

"There's no ship on Saturday, sir." He replied smartly.
"But I can go on Friday."

Major Panzera peered down into the howitzer shelter from
the rim of the hollow.

"Ready for blasting, sir," he informed his commander. The
two men returned to Cannon Kopje under the luminous red
dusk sky, tinged with a band of pale egg-shell green. The first
stars of the African night twinkled high above the gaunt black
silhouettes of the sleeping kopjes. An officer strolled over to
an ant-bear hole and introduced a stick of dynamite. He lit the
fuse and ran for cover. The charge went off with a splendid
roar and an impressive cloud of dust, from which emerged a
farmer on a bike. He pedaled off as hard as he could towards
the Boer lines. With a bit of luck he would spread stories about
mines buried everywhere. In fact the mysterious boxes had
nothing more dangerous in them than sand.

The star-studded African night descended abruptly on the
besieged town and with it the possibility of an attack under
cover of darkness. It had happened before. Guided by a British deserter, a Boer force had followed the path beside the
Molopo River to where it entered the native African village
and set fire to the huts. To forestall this happening again,
Baden-Powell had enlisted the help of an expert on acetylene
lighting. Between them they had devised a portable search-
light made out of a biscuit tin nailed to the top of a pole. It
could be turned on for a few seconds at one spot and then
rushed off to another for a few flashes and so on all round the
perimeter. From a distance the effect was stunning.

Back at HQ, Baden-Powell stretched out in an easy chair
on the verandah and tried to relax. He listened to the sound

of his batman pouring him a drink and the sharp clink of the bottle against the rim of the glass. Like Rhodes he loved the night, in a way only silent solitary men can love. Rumors circulated about his suppressed homosexuality, but he shrugged them off. He yearned only for the peace and quietude of the night, when he could escape from the dusty bustle of the besieged town onto the moonless veldt, an unobtrusive spectator in mystical communion with nature.

He caught sight of a piece of paper on the floor, Rhodes' last message from Kimberley, and leant over to pick it up.

"Colonel Kekewick is worked off his legs, so I am sending you a request for information as to your position. Let me know briefly how long your foodstuffs and forage will last, the state of your health and water supply. How is the shelling affecting you? What are your losses to date? As to ourselves here in Kimberley, we can just hold our own but cannot relieve you. I'm rather afraid the military authorities in Cape Town think that we can hold out for ever! If it is otherwise with you, you should pocket your pride and tell them the contrary." Unknown to either man, British forces commanded by Colonel Mahon had already started to move north. Among them was one of Baden-Powell's brothers.

The colonel whistled a few more bars of Verdi and fidgeted with the last ultimatum he had received from the Boer commander inviting him to surrender. He asked his ADC for the latest casualty list: 326 soldiers and 476 civilians dead in the shelling, fifty percent of his officers wounded. Well, the game wasn't over yet! They wouldn't be beaten by a few rotten Boer shells! He turned to Major Panzera.

"What are the chances of getting a reply through to General Cronje tonight?"

"Pretty good, I think, sir."

"Send me a messenger at once then." He pulled his notebook across the table and hastily scribbled a message. In less than an hour the Boer General's ADC, Sarel Eloff, the grandson of President Kruger, held it to the flickering petrol lamp. After eight months' siege everyone expected surrender. They were wrong. Baden-Powell had written: 'Makeking, in the game it is playing at present, is 210 not out against the bowling of Cronje, Snyman and Eloff. Don't you think you'd better change the bowling?' Two days later, Cronje ordered the withdrawal of six thousand Boers, leaving Snyman to carry on the siege with the remaining three thousand militia.

The 'cricket story' rapidly went the rounds back in Cape Town. Henry Juta failed to keep his hilarity hidden whenever he heard the story. His wife showed more concern for the dead and wounded.

"Really, Tim! I do wish you wouldn't make your indifference to the suffering of our men so obvious in front of the children." Her husband took the rebuff in silence. He cast a rapid glance across the lunch table at Luia and Jan. Visibly they had a better sense of humor than their mother. Helen Juta worked tirelessly for the War Cause. The shiploads of fashionable London ladies who had invaded the Cape to 'care for' the wounded infuriated her. Their caring consisted mostly of parading the streets in the latest Paris dresses and having dubious affairs with the overworked medical officers. It put Helen Juta quite out of temper.

"And I do think Mrs. Baggot might try and hide her very conspicuous partiality for Edward Tooth a bit better. I wonder she dares to be seen with him in public!" She straightened her shoulders, perhaps hoping to add a few inches to the height of her indignation. In fact her back gave her considerable pain from stooping so constantly over hospital beds. Her aristocratic blood relegated such fickle females as Elizabeth Baggot to the portals of purgatory. Henry Juta made a vague gesture with his hands.

"Come now, Birdie. I'm sure Dr. Tooth has enough problems with his patients without being held to account for his private life also." Helen Juta's face assumed its wounded look.

"I wasn't blaming Dr. Tooth", she objected. But she did blame him. She blamed him for being so affable and familiar with women like Elizabeth Baggot and Lady

Cavendish-Bentick in their huge floppy Paris hats and wispy scarves. She blamed him for taking her for granted, president of the Hospital Board and the Guild of Loyal Women. Now she had a new project in mind: the South African Women's Industrial Union. It would organize and dispose of work which could be done by poor women in their own homes. It would provide relief for a number of women who otherwise could find no outlet for their work. Her husband looked upon the project with benevolent misgiving.

"Is your Union prepared to guarantee that the work will be done by these women and done well too?" he enquired. "What sort of work do you have in mind?" Helen Juta tapped her foot impatiently under the table.

"Work of all kinds," she expostulated. "Mending worn clothing, for example. And the rates are really very reasonable. Too low for the work done. It's a question of humanity. The difference between self-respect and charity."

Luia listened to these scraps of conversation between her parents with a growing consciousness of their significance. With her three sisters away at boarding school in England and Jan under the ubiquitous eye of his tutor, Luia had stepped into the role of 'second in command' to her mother. Together they paid daily visits to the Rosebank Hospital Camp three miles away from 'Mon Desir'. An amoeboid sprawl of rain-marked, disinfectant-fetid canvas tents, it seemed hardly a place for a nine year-old girl, but with the Victorian gift for pure paradox, Helen Juta trailed her sensitive daughter through the aisles of suffering, conscious only that she did her duty to humanity. Under the worn yellowing sun-filtered canvas in the sweet pervasive air, Luia was made to stand on a wooden crate and sing to the long lines of mutilated heroes. 'Who are the lads who have made her glorious? Who are the lads who have made Britain's fame? It's the lads of the red white and blue, me boys. It's the lads of the red white and blue!"

After singing the song a dozen times, Luia marched round the depressing ward with a brimming basket of yellow and purple grapes. She moved from bed to bed, past blank vacant eyes and amputated limbs, only partially grasping the fear and consternation in those pain-weary faces. She had seen such fear in faces before. As a baby, Jan had almost died of pleurisy. The whole house had fallen under the mesmerizing mantle of potential death. In the silent schoolroom no one concentrated on their lessons. Helpless to assuage her son's condition or even check his fever, Helen Juta wandered despairingly among her lilies. That cloud had been lifted by Sir Edmund Stevenson, the surgeon who attended Cecil Rhodes the day of his death. He performed the operation on the baby's left lung in the house. While servants scrubbed the table, boiled water and prepared clean towels, the surgeon mounted the great teak staircase to the schoolroom. Despite his appeasing words and his suggestions that the other children pray to God to guide his scalpel, it was the silence that Luia remembered most, the same silence of fearful expectation; in the house, in the surgeon's eyes and the eyes of the two hundred mutilated men dying on blood-stained camp beds, while a nine year-old girl on a wooden crate sang in their praise, those lost lads of the red white and blue.

Henry Juta folded his monographed linen napkin at the side of his plate. He thought about risking a further remark on Baden-Powell's sense of humor but the hall clock struck two o'clock and brought him back to earth. Little time remained for his Saturday inspection of the gardens before setting out for Simonstown. Noticing him take out his watch, Helen Juta rang the bell for the butler. The filtered rays of the afternoon sun shone like fragments of a shattered rainbow through the tinted panes of the leaded windows in their massive teak mullions. They illuminated the ornately-carved walnut mantelpiece with its frieze of old curiously-patterned Dutch tiles lining the open fireplace.

The butler appeared with the dessert, an 'omlette surprise' that never failed to arouse the enthusiasm of the two youngest Jutas. This Saturday, however, they had a special reason to be excited. Their father was taking them to visit the

'Discovery', anchored in Simonstown Bay for a day or two on its way to the South Atlantic. Henry Juta had prepared the adventure.

"Antartica," he explained, as the train steamed south down the fertile Leesbeck Valley, "is a circular continent beyond the stormiest ocean in the world, a continent covered by a mile-thick mantel of ice. Only along the coasts can the rugged mountain ranges emerge from the ice cap. On the gravel beaches live undisturbed thousands of penguins and seals." They saw the famous ship at once from the train window. It lay at anchor, a short distance from shore, in the midst of a dozen smaller vessels, ferrying visitors or supplies on board. A ring of rugged ridges framed the high-masted black-timbered ship. Whitewashed naval buildings lined the beach. A recent landslide scarred the hillside behind the town. A fan of exposed shale reflected the spring sun. Henry Juta lowered the carriage window at the risk of getting soot in his eyes and pointed.

"The 'Discovery' was especially built for the work in hand, strong enough to withstand the ice pressure over the long winter months." In fact the ship would remain two years trapped in the ice. "One of the tasks facing the expedition is the exploration of the Magnetic Pole. So there is nothing metallic on board. A magnet will attract iron, even though the two are not in contact." Luia gazed at the imposing ship at anchor and marveled. Even the nails had been replaced by wooded plugs.

"Are we going to meet the Admiral?" she wondered, as the train squealed to a halt along the platform. Her father stood by the carriage door and looked for the shore party that would row them out to the 'Discovery'.

"Commander Scott isn't an admiral yet", he corrected. "Nevertheless, he has been chosen for this mission, as being the most suited to the job." The cloud of hissing steam from the locomotive dispersed in the sea breeze to reveal a smart clean-shaven naval officer in an impeccable white uniform. Commander Robert Falcon Scott had come in person to meet the Speaker of the Cape House and his children. He looked extremely young to command such an expedition. In fact he was only thirty-two and his appointment had raised some opposition. There had been committee battles over the scope of Scott's responsibilities. The Royal Society had tried to impose one of their own scientists as leader. In the end Scott had been chosen, despite an almost total lack of Antarctic experience and very little special training. Scott's insistence on Royal Navy formalities created uneasy relations with the merchant navy members of the expedition. As they rowed out to the anchorage Scott outlined his mission to the barrister.

"Of course, we're not going completely in the dark," he explained. "The Russians established a base at Cape Adare two years ago. They even managed to sail as far as the Ross Ice Shelf, a two hundred mile long vertical ice cliff, but they found it had shifted considerably since James Ross first discovered it in 1842. Borchgrevink, the Russian expedition leader, skied south to what he calculated to be 78°. We hope to do better than that!" he added. The oars creaked and the water slapped the moving hull. Luia trailed an arm in the clear turquoise water. Bands of brightly-colored fish darted off at right angles to the wake. At last they pulled alongside the 'Discovery' and Scott reached for the rope ladder. On deck a line of naval cadets stood smartly to attention. Dressed in her number one sailor suit, Luia felt quite at home and recalled a recent music hall song the laundry girls had taught her behind her parents' back: 'All the nice girls love a sailor, all the nice girls love a tar, for there's something about a sailor. Well, you know what sailors are!' She found herself humming the tune as she passed along the line of cadets and blushed. Scott led his guests to the poop deck.

"I don't suppose this war with the Boers has affected you too much down here," he remarked. Henry Juta winced. Apart from forcing his allegiances to breaking point and overburdening his conscience, no, the war hadn't affected him much! The outward calm of 'Mon Desir' remained undisturbed. The number of naval and military visitors had increased. His wife spent more time away from home on her 'missions.' Miraculously he had managed to stay friends with both William Schreiner and Cecil Rhodes, who had returned from the besieged Kimberley and sailed immediately for England. It was to be his last visit to the country of his birth. Lord Roberts, in charge of the relief of both Kimberley and Ladysmith had made Rhodes a colonel and praised his behavior during the siege, while condemning Kekewick for having obstructed the millionaire's plans. Rhodes pretended to have forgotten who the unfortunate Kekewick was.

"You don't remember the man who cleans your boots," he remarked. Willie Schreiner, unable to accept the British demands for a full penalty in the now-probable event of a total Boer defeat, had resigned as Prime Minister. His last words in office reflected his disenchantment:

"I had hoped to steer the ship of the Colony into the port of peace, but as I must hand her over to another pilot, I wish him a good voyage. She has not been hulled, though her tackle has been damaged here and there." For his friend Henry Juta he would always be remembered as incorruptible with an unblemished integrity and loyalty. As he paced the deck of 'Discovery' with Scott, his thoughts turned to another past friend he had not been able to retain. Jan Smuts had stayed in Johannesburg, trying to hold together a crumbling Transvaal. President Kruger had fled to Switzerland to die in exile on the shores of Lac Leman. Smuts understood that it all came down to a question of obligation.

"If humanity did not meet its obligations and fulfill its tasks, accept the responsibilities that the universe thrust upon it, humanity would be replaced, just as other animal species that have failed to survive. Take yourself, Juta," he wrote in his last letter to Henry Juta. "You are a whole. Take myself. I am a whole. We both possess a certain inwardness of spirit and other supplementary characteristics that we call the personality. We also have a body, and all the time we remain in touch with something beyond the body. We have a vision that extends to the stars. We have a memory that takes us back over the ages as far as there are records and sometimes farther. Any whole has infinite ramifications." As he remembered the familiar words, Henry Juta heard the soft burred voice, pictured the startling blue eyes that looked straight at you and seemed to be reading the small print at the back of your mind. The sentences came out as staccato phrases. Smuts gave the impression that he had no wish to waste his breath on unnecessary verbal displays. The letter had ended:

"I don't say that the sun and the moon and the stars and the ages are all part of my personality. That would be going too far. There must be limits. I like to think of the word 'field'. Every whole has its field and these fields interpenetrate each other. It is this intermingling of fields that forms the creative elements of our universe. I don't believe that we human beings are the same. I believe there will be evolved far higher forms of spiritual wholes than we see before us today. We shall not remain in the front rank of Creation."

While Scott and Juta paced the deck discussing skis and dogs and Scott's preference for man-hauling, the practice of propelling sledges by manpower alone, Luia sat in the sun against a poop deck railing and thumbed through a slim leather-bound volume that the commander had taken from his pocket and suggested she might like to read to pass the time. It was his personal copy of James Ross' 'A Voyage of Discovery and Research to Southern and Antarctic Regions' published in 1847 after his return from four years in Antarctica aboard the 'Erebus'. Scott had underlined certain passages from Ross' diary which immediately attracted Luia's attention:

"... an ocean of rolling fragments of ice, hard as floating rocks of granite, which are dashed against us by waves with such violence that our masts quiver. There seems to be but little probability of our ships holding together much longer, so frequent and violent are the shocks they sustain." As the two ships sailed south, Ross saw a low white line "extending from its eastern extreme point as far as the eye could discern. It represented an extraordinary appearance, gradually increasing in height, as we got nearer to it, and proving at length to be a perpendicular cliff of ice, level at the top and without any fissures or promontories on its seaward side. We might with equal chance of success try and sail through the cliffs of Dover as penetrate such a mass." He named it the Victoria Barrier, later changed to the Ross Ice Shelf.

The weather had remained a constant problem. Ross spent much of the southern summer frustrated by his efforts to find a route through the pack ice. Then in the darkness on March 12 an enormous iceberg loomed directly ahead. The ship was immediately hauled to the wind on the port tack, but at the same moment the second vessel, 'Terror', sped down on them under top sails and it was impossible for her to clear both the iceberg and 'Erebus'. A collision was inevitable.

"We instantly hove all aback to diminish the violence of the shock, but the concussion when she struck us was such as to throw everyone off his feet. Our bowsprit, foretopmast and other smaller spars, were carried away. The ships, hanging together, entangled by their rigging and dashing against each other with fearful violence, were falling down upon the weather face of the lofty berg under our lee, against which the waves were breaking and foaming to near the summit of the perpendicular cliffs. Sometimes she rose high above us, almost exposing her keel to view, and again descended as we in our turn rose to the top of the wave. The crashing of the breaking upperworks and boats increased the horror of the scene. Disabled, we drifted onto the berg so close that the waves striking it threw back their spray into the ship."

"You had better stop reading, young lady, or you'll be having nightmares for a week." Commander Scott removed the book from Luia's hands and turned to her father. "Of course, the 'Erebus' and 'Terror' were bomb vessels, a very unusual type of warship named after the mortar bombs they were designed to fire and constructed with extremely strong hulls to withstand the recoil of the mortars. They proved to be of great value in the thick ice."

A week later the Discovery Expedition set sail for Tasmania. After two winters in Antarctica it would take the combined efforts of two relief ships and the use of explosives to free Scott's ship from the ice. Luia's visit ended with a parting gift from the Commander of a rating's hat with 'Discovery' on the ribbon. She perched it on the back of her head as the train rumbled back along the coast towards Muizenberg. A south-easterly wind had risen and already the flat top of Table Mountain had disappeared under the thick moist 'tablecloth'. It soaked the deeply dissected plateau with its luxuriant profusion of orchids and proteas. Only lower down below the rim of sandstone cliffs the forests of silver pines and ironwood radiated the glow of falling dusk. Luia adjusted the hat on her head, straightened the ribbon and hummed to herself.

"All the nice girls love a sailor; all the nice girls love a tar."

CHAPTER . . .

7

"Well, today's the day." William Schreiner spoke across the breakfast table to his wife, the sister of William Reitz, State Secretary of the South African Republic, formerly the Transvaal. Like her renowned brother, Fanny had been born into a family of twelve and raised on their father's model farm at Rhenosterfontein on the banks of the Breederivier. She admired her brother immensely. An important figure in Afrikaner cultural life, William was a popular personality with a judicial career that lasted over forty-five years. Trained as a lawyer, he had soon made a name for himself, due to his sharp legal mind and his social intelligence. He was one of the first Afrikaners to actively develop a 'Bantu policy', in philosophy and terminology, going beyond contemporary ideas on segregation between white and black. As State Secretary of the South African Republic he ordered that all correspondence with the government should be in Dutch. Originally praised by the British for his diplomatic courtesy, their attitude quickly changed when they understood that Reitz actively promoted Transvaal independence. The British army had now marched on Pretoria and the Boer government forced to flee the capital. Over the next two years the seat would be relocated sixty-two times.

Fanny Schreiner noted the slightly malicious twinkle in her husband's eye as he smoothed his substantial beard, still dark over the upper lip but completely gray over the chin and jowls. He wore his usual heavy brown tweed suit. He still hadn't fully come to terms with the way his anti-war stance had forced him to resign as Prime Minister. Today, however, he wanted to enjoy himself. The trial of Princess

Radziwill opened at Kalk Bay police court. If he looked out of his window he could see the building half a mile down the coast road. He had looked out of the window. He hadn't stopped looking out of the window since the early morning train from Cape Town had disgorged its load of fashionable ladies with official invitations to the trial. The authorities had ransacked the village for enough chairs to seat them all.

Catherine Radziwill had to face charges of forgery and embezzlement. She had signed Rhodes' name on a total of £23,000 worth of promissory notes. Rhodes had appeared in court in February, looking very ill and breathing with great difficulty, to swear that he had never signed a single note. The Princess claimed he had, but few people believed a word she said any more. They shrugged her off with a giggle as being an adventuress in desperate need of funds. Rhodes' enemies, however, had little interest in the forged bills. The Princess claimed to have in her possession documents that Rhodes would dearly like to recover. Rumors circulated asserting that they concerned the missing wires sent to Rhodes from London prior to the disastrous Jameson Raid, wires that proved the complicity of Lord Milner and the British cabinet. The charges against her now included blackmail. All Cape Town society waited impatiently for the scandalously sensational trial to open.

Schreiner observed the crowd gathering outside the police station with the detached curiosity of a lawyer. Since his resignation, he had retired from public life. He had dropped out of most of the clubs and societies he once frequented, even the Civil Service Club. The war with the Boer republics and his failure to secure a peaceful settlement had destroyed his confidence in himself and humanity. Crowds had booed and stoned him for his anti-war beliefs. Someone had even fired a pistol at him as he strolled in his garden. He took it all with a pessimistic passiveness and went back to his law practice, as though he had never laid it aside to dabble in politics.

He still loved to fish off the rocks at Splash Point with Henry Juta. A few weeks before he had landed a hundred pound kabeljauw. Otherwise his life had sunk back into a regulated ritual: each morning he set off for the office with bulging bag, his battered felt hat pulled over his eyes. He halted briefly at Kelvin Grove to feed the tame springbok with bread and salt from his pocket, with Pat, his Irish terrier, gamboling round his feet. He commuted to town by train and during the return journey he filled in the time by solving chess problems. In all weathers Pat waited at the station gate to carry his stick and the evening edition of the 'Argos'. Weekends passed indolently at the St. James cottage. All in all he realized he had become a perfect little bourgeois and the thought riled him.

He turned back to the window. The crowd down the road had thickened and completely masked the entrance to the court.

"Aren't you sorry you're not going, dear?" Schreiner shrugged at the teasing tone in his wife's question. He didn't reply. He had no invitation. Unlike Henry Juta, who was Rhodes' counsel, he had no official function to perform. He opened the curtains wider. Beyond Dalebrook a second crowd had assembled outside the house the Princess had rented, a pretentious villa with huge overhanging gables, rather like a Swiss chalet but much bigger. People said that the Princess had paid no rent for seven months. Behind the villa along the rock-bound beach a high sea roared and hissed. Vaporous clouds of spume flew across the narrow strip of salt marsh as far as the road. Shafts of sunlight transformed the suspended droplets into miniature rainbows.

Dr. Jameson hurried past in the direction of Muizenberg with his typical elastic tread and slightly swinging gait, to sit with Rhodes and await the verdict. The millionaire's fatal heart disease had made rapid progress. Still a relatively young man, he had led a clean healthy virtuous open-air life. In all his habits he had been temperate and frugal, but he had never spared himself, never taken care of himself and no woman's love had ever watched over him. Fanny Schreiner noticed Jameson and snorted.

"Just like his master! He's no South African!" Her remark irritated Schreiner.

"We're all South Africans!" he snapped. "Only the man who stubbornly refuses to make himself at home here is an Uitlander." In fact Schreiner had come to be quite fond of the eccentric Scottish doctor who was to become Cape Prime Minister two years later. Though impulsive and often over-confident, 'Doctor Jim' remained extremely popular for his charm, intelligence and selfless loyalty. Master of the art of persuasion, Jameson possessed an unparallel power of con-centration, logical reasoning and rapid diagnosis. Schreiner maintained his position.

"Take a man at his word," he insisted, "and judge a man by his acts. If this country is to fulfill its destiny, it must be through the willing acceptance of willing workers towards the great end, without this perpetual revival of the echo of past controversies, of the bitterness of past differences. Is there to be no room for repentance?" Fanny Schreiner threw up her hands.

"O God! Hoor die man!" They both laughed. Along the dusty sun-baked road Jameson had reached the Bailey's house. He realized how much he had changed since the fate-ful raid. Five months in prison with its consequent illness had made him cautious. He could now appreciate the untold damage he had inflicted on the British cause in South Africa as well as ruining his friend's political career. He had taken up the struggle for South African federation and been elected Member of Parliament for Kimberley. Nobody doubted that on Rhodes' death he would succeed him as leader of the Cape Progressive party. With so much to lose, there would be no more fireworks from 'Dr. Jim'.

Edith Rhodes sat on the rabbit-hutch verandah in con-versation with Mrs. Carter, the housekeeper. As Jameson climbed the uneven wooden steps, a brightly-striped rock lizard darted under his feet into a crack in the loose cement. The two women acknowledged Jameson's greeting and went on with their reminiscences of the earlier days in the

Muizenberg cottage. The Bailey and Juta girls would call in after a day on the beach or after the races at Kenilworth with the large lace patterns of their cotton frocks burnt into the skin. Mrs. Carter would rub their burnt skin with fresh cream in the hope that by evening the marks would have disappeared and the girls could face their dance partners at the Hunt Ball without blushing.

Rhodes sat on his bed at the open window, hoping to catch the sea breeze. Tormented by the stifling heat and the Princess's persecution, he had returned early from his last visit to England to give evidence and then retire to the seclusion of the beach cottage to die. When Jameson entered, the dying man sat with one leg on the floor and the other akimbo in front of him on the bed. Alternatively he gasped for breath or dropped his heavy head so low that his chin almost touched his chest. Opposite him sat a ferrety-faced woman with a sallow complexion but bright darting eyes. She wore a man's veldt jacket buckled at the waist and a wide-brimmed felt hat. One of the few women who understood Rhodes well enough to become a friend, Flora Shaw was Colonial Editor for 'The Times' newspaper, the post that Catherine Radziwill once sought to fill. Already regarded as one of the greatest journalists of her time, specializing in politics and economics, Flora Shaw believed, like Rhodes, that the vast empty spaces of Africa only awaited energetic English settlers. She believed in the positive benefits of the British Empire. She had written five novels and a little-known aspect of her prominent career was that when she first started writing, she tried to disguise the fact that she was a woman. Later she was so highly regarded that it no longer mattered and she wrote openly as Flora Shaw. In less than a year she would marry Sir Frederick Lugard, a colonial administrator, later to become Governor of Hong Kong.

"Really, Prime Minister!" she exclaimed. "You appear to me, but don't imagine that I'm infallible as a judge of character, to seek nothing for yourself. You care nothing for money, or place, or power, except in so far as they are a necessity for the accomplishment of the national ideas for which you live. You have no personal life whatsoever." Jameson wanted to interpose between the prying reporter and the man he admired so much for his bravery, cheerfulness and unselfishness. A few days from certain death, he looked determined, dignified and masterful still. Rhodes raised his hand to stop the doctor interfering.

"When I was a young man," he wheezed, "and ought to have married, when I was in the mood, so to speak, I was so poor that I couldn't afford it. And now, since I am richer, well, upon my soul, I haven't had the time to think about it." Another choking fit doubled him over, his pale flabby face purple, the muscles of his neck taut as iron bands as he struggled for breath. Jameson waited for the fit to pass and handed him the letter he had received that morning from Catherine Radziwill. A maid had watched for him and slipped out by the back gate to intercept him with the message. Rhodes tore open the envelope.

"Why, this is addressed to you, Jameson," he muttered testily. Jameson shrugged and closed his heavy drooping eyelids.

"Makes no odds," he said. "You read it. I want nothing to do with the woman." He settled on the window sill and watched a group of children driving a hoop down the sandy lane. Rhodes began the letter.

"Dear Dr. Jameson. As you will have learned through the papers, I have paid Mr. Louw's bill."

"He can be damned thankful," cut in the doctor from the window. "What kind of a fool lends money to a person he has never seen and from whom he demands no guarantees?" Rhodes lifted the letter and continued to read.

"Had you done me the pleasure of calling on me as I requested you to, I would have told you that all I desired was Mr. Rhodes' counsel, not his opposition to the request for postponement of the trial. The money was paid on Monday." Rhodes threw the letter on the floor. "The devil it was!" he exclaimed with such force that both Flora Shaw and Jameson jumped up. Only the doctor could guess at the cause of his friend's astonishment. Tom Louw was one of Rhodes' closest associates. The loan of £2,000 without guarantee had been engineered by Rhodes himself, on the assumption that the Princess would be unable to repay it, would be taken to court and definitively discredited. Consequently any incriminating documents she might later produce would be subject to the highest suspicion. Somehow, against all odds, Catherine had found the money to repay Louw.

Conscious of the newspaper correspondent's presence, Rhodes calmed down, picked up the fallen letter and continued the lecture. "After the abominable lies Mr. Rhodes told in court, neither he nor you will wonder that I tell you that I mean to take strong measures to prove he repeated in the Supreme Court his experiments before the Select Committee of the House of Commons. In one case he perjured himself to save Mr. Chamberlain. In the second he did so to dishonor a woman who had fought his battles and been his true friend. Well, I shall show that I can bite!" Rhodes laughed a little hysterically. He had dealt with many people in his long political career, but never with persecution from a woman of such baleful and obstinate character. She had been judged by the Attorney-General himself and committed for trial as a common forger and intriguer, but she still persisted in her lies. She wanted revenge because he had openly ignored her, shunned her marriage proposal, paid her to leave the country. She had returned to push him into his grave. She had forced him to return to Cape Town in the hot season. She knew that the doctors had warned him that his heart condition was serious. Instead of grouse shooting in the cold dry Scottish hills round Rannoch Lodge, he had to swelter and suffocate in a South African heat wave.

Flora Shaw realized at once that whatever hold the Princess had over Rhodes, he considered it important enough to gamble with his life in order to silence her. Since his return from England, Catherine haunted the lane outside the Muizenberg cottage. For hours on end she lurked among the bushes or stood under her parasol staring at his verandah, so that he no longer dared sit out there and enjoy the breezes.

"Damn the woman!" Rhodes exploded. "What am I to do, Jameson?" The doctor, who habitually wrapped himself in a clock of cynicism, never hid from his friends the truth, as he saw it.

"You've no alternative," he replied with decided firmness. His remarkably broad brow and prominent nose showed determination. "Prosecute the woman for forgery." Obviously reluctant to do that, Rhodes pulled a wry face. He wanted no publicity. Unlike Jameson, he didn't approve entirely of subordinating personal considerations to the work in hand. He was less logical and rapid in grasping a situation than the doctor.

"As you have already declared the bills to be forgeries, you have no alternative," repeated Jameson. Rhodes capitulated. He was no match for 'Dr.Jim'. After the disastrous Raid, he had told Flora Shaw: "Whatever one feels about Jameson or his projects when he is not there, one cannot help falling for the man in his presence. People attach themselves to him with extraordinary fervor, the more extraordinary because he makes no effort to feed it. He affects an attitude of tough cynicism towards life, literature and any articulate form of idealism."

Jameson stood with his back to the window, his imposing head with its receding hairline tilted a little to one side. He was carefully dressed in a dark frock coat and trousers, a spotless white necktie and pale gray gloves. He disapproved of Rhodes' reluctance to prosecute Princess Radziwill because he knew why. Rhodes had a weakness for royalty. As he had pointed out to the Supreme Court, Catherine had once served as maid of honor to the Empress of Prussia.

At that moment the deposed maid of honor sat forlornly in her bedroom. On each side of the sumptuous crimson velvet and damask curtains, which she had not yet paid for, gold-framed prints of European royalty, faded and fantastic like her own universe, covered the walls. Through the window she contemplated the blinding silver expanse of False Bay. A smeared trail of brown smoke on the horizon marked the passage of a liner coasting north to Durban and India. A wardrobe door hung open, displaying dozens of elegant dresses from every part of Europe, dresses that had witnessed the chandelier glitter and waxed parquet of ballrooms in Berlin and Moscow, in London, in Saint Petersburg and Paris.

Now that she faced public trial and possible internment, Catherine had begun to think twice about showing how hard she could bite. She would put on a brave face, but the time had come for some amateur theatricals. Her maid kept her informed of the situation outside the police station, the waiting, gossip-mongering crowd. Well, she had no intention of gratifying their thirst for scandal by appearing in court. She leaned across the bed and tugged torpidly at a bunch of grapes in a blue Delft bowl on the bedside table. Standing stiffly to attention at the foot of the bed, Inspector George Easton of the C.I.D. listened long-sufferingly to her ranting and claims of sudden indisposition. Better than the theatre, he was thinking!

"I was taken ill the other day," the Princess explained, "just as I was about to start for town to attend the sitting of the Supreme Court. I am more than sorry that I was thus prevented from challenging some of the most extraordinary statements made by Mr. Rhodes in court that morning." She stretched out a slender white arm towards a Pekinese, curled up on a red silk cushion on the rug. The top of her dressing gown parted slightly, revealing the folds of loose skin on her neck and a brief glimpse of breasts that had once been her pride. Inspector Easton noticed the powder applied thickly to her cheeks to give them a ghostly pallor.

"One single statement would have made me jump to my feet," she exclaimed dramatically in a tone of self-righteous grief. "It is curious that Mr. Rhodes at one time wished me to leave the country," she added. Easton smothered the desire to smile. He had been in court that day and remembered

Rhodes' answer to the question as to whether he had ever given the Princess money.

"I paid her bills if she would leave the country. But she came back!" A titter had rippled through the courtroom. Catherine saw the germ of a smile on the policeman's face.

"What interest could Mr. Rhodes have had in my going or staying in South Africa," she snapped, "if his acquaintance with me was so slight?" Her black eyes dared him to suggest that it was because she had driven him to distraction with the daily visits and demands for help. Inspector Easton glanced at his watch. Something had to be done.

"I must ask you to accompany me to Kalk Bay police station," he said in a firm but unconvincing voice. He wondered how he was going to overlook the fact that his arrest warrant concerned a princess propped up in bed in her dressing gown with a Pekinese. Catherine tossed her head. A switch of thick black hair slipped over her bare shoulder.

"Lady Macbeth in person," thought Easton, scratching his ear. Catherine showed no signs of moving.

"I come of a strong clever and brave race, Inspector," she informed him with a disdainful smile. "We Poles are famous for our personal courage and remarkable intelligence. The Empress, however, always disliked me and made no bones about it. I was far too independent for her." She picked up the book she had been reading before the interview and sank back into the pile of pillows. Easton saluted smartly and left the room. If the Princess would not come to the court, the court would come to the Princess.

In his paneled study at 'Mon Desir', Henry Juta pursed his lips and inhaled the fumes of his brandy. In the deep leather armchair opposite him Colonel Baden-Powell lifted his own glass in a toast. Since the relief of Mafeking, he had taken part in the campaign to capture the illusive Boer commander, Christiaan de Wet, the most formidable leader of the Boers in their guerilla warfare. At the outbreak of war, De Wet left his farm to harass the British, escaping only by the narrowest

margin of safety from the columns which attempted to sur-
round him, annihilating isolated British posts and striking
heavily wherever he could. He had so far skillfully evaded
every attempt to capture him. Baden-Powell had then worked
on the reconstruction of the railway to Pretoria, organiz-
ing teams of oxen to haul the trains. He had founded the
South African Constabulary. For this complicated task, Cecil
Rhodes had given him a tranquil wing in Groote Schuur as
an office. Henry Juta put down his glass.

"We had to pack up everything in the police station and
move down the road," he said, "into her own drawing-room!
She faced us like a tigress at bay and then pretended to
faint." The dignified barrister tried unsuccessfully to hide the
mixture of mirth and indignation at the Princess's scheming.
Somewhere one had to draw the line between chivalry and
legality. A common shop-lifter would have been brought to
the station by force. Baden-Powell nodded in agreement. He
watched a group of colored workmen weeding the croquet
lawn.

"Nevertheless, you have to admire her nerve," he confessed. The scene appealed to his sense of adventure and individual initiative. Henry Juta, who had officially chaired the
hearing, hesitated before replying.

"Criminal though she undoubtedly is, I felt more respect
for the Princess than I did for all those gossiping over-dressed
town ladies, as they scrambled and shoved into the half-court,
half-drawing room to secure the best seats on the sofas and
armchairs. And to gaze at what? A heavily-powdered face
propped up with cushions on an improvised camp bed!"

The two men lapsed into a silence, broken only by the
subdued whirr of a lawn-mower and the steady rhythmic tick
of the grandfather clock in the hall. In the pine wood Luia
and Jan chased each other among the trees with screams of
exaltation. Henry Juta smiled. The sounds reminded him of
Baden-Powell's purpose in visiting him.

"Tell me exactly what sort of men you are looking for?"
he asked. Baden-Powell prepared to launch into his favorite

topic. Although he had not taken much notice of them during the siege, he had been impressed with the courage of the youngsters in the cadet corps and the calm with which they had performed their tasks. He needed the same qualities for the new South African Constabulary.

"Intelligent young fellows who can use their wits, stay calm and who haven't been drilled into soulless machines," he explained. "Men who have made mistakes. I reckon that every man makes a mistake some time or other in his career. Many of my men will have made their mistakes and are therefore all the more likely not to do so in the future. Of course, it's staking all on an uncertain gamble." A bout of coughing forced him to stop. Inwardly he cursed his doctor who had secretly written to his mother in England that he suspected bronchitis. Now he had to cope with endless letters pleading with him to seek sick leave and come home. Henry Juta knew that the colonel maintained an extensive correspondence with his widowed mother. He attributed his success entirely to the way she had brought up her family alone.

Luia and Jan were now squabbling noisily under the window. Henry Juta shook his head.

"I rather suspect that the hero of Mafeking is being waited for," he remarked. "I hope you weren't rash enough to promise them anything." Baden-Powell flushed like a guilty schoolboy.

"Oh, I just said we might go up the hill for a bit of scouting," he replied evasively. He leaned forward to smell a loaded branch of camellia blossoms in a vase on the table. "Exquisite!"

"Don't let them tire you out," insisted Juta. At the Club people talked about how the popular hero was working himself towards a breakdown. Baden-Powell snorted.

"After Eloff and his merry men? Not much chance of that!" He jumped briskly to his feet, straightened his uniform and reached for his bush hat. The two men stepped out of the French windows onto the flagged terrace. A pair of collared turtle doves rose from the steep slate roof. Their soft purring coo followed them into the pines. The bright overhead sun cast short sharp shadows through the dark leathery leaves of the solitary valonia oak. The large globular acorn cups swung in clusters round the thick fissured trunk.

Baden-Powell strode out onto the gravel drive, tying the leather strap of his bush hat under his chin.

"What's it to be, then?" he enquired.

"Scouts!" came the two replies in unison. The colonel wondered if their father grasped just how much construc-tive information he gleaned simply from playing his games with the children, information he could later apply to his schemes for youth training. Children of that age possessed a spontaneous curiosity, an instinctive gift for simple com-mon sense, lost with the advent of adolescence. He raised a warning hand.

"First I must see if you qualify for that," he said, smooth-ing his thick mustache. The two children knew what to ex-pect. They called it 'Kim's game', because it reminded them of the game Kim had to play on Lurgan Sahib's verandah in Simla with the Hindu boy. Kim called it the 'Jewel game'. They had to look at a tray of stones for ten seconds and then describe everything in detail. The Hindu boy got them all right every time. Baden-Powell turned to Luia first, being the eldest.

"Who was the third person you saw today?" She didn't have to think long.

"Theal!" she cried assertively. Theal was the Danish un-der-nurse. Luia had seen her at the gate waving to a regi-ment of new troops passing down Main Road on their way to the barracks. She had overheard the habitual exchange of gallantries.

"Hello, baby! How's the nurse?" and then "Hello, nurse! How's the baby?" The laughter that followed made little sense to Luia. What baby were they referring to? There were practically no more children at 'Mon Desir'. Her two eldest sisters had already finished boarding school in England and were studying music in Berlin and Paris. Luia's childhood too neared the end. In another year she would be waving goodbye to Cape Town from the deck of a home-bound liner. Only the frail sensitive Jan would remain to haunt the 'museum' and wander alone in the Newlands woods. In families like hers, tradition ruled over sentiment. After a European education, few Cape children of British origin returned to settle in the land of their birth. Many never set foot on African soil again. The Dutch were different. Born on farms away on the veldt, they came from the land itself and nearly always returned to the land. It was easy to understand why they considered themselves the real South Africans and the British merely colonizing parasites.

"The third person I saw was Captain Tupman," interceded Jan shrilly. "He was talking to Mrs. Palmer. She was complaining that his men had been pulling branches off the silver trees in the park to feed the donkey." He finished his report in a wild breathless rush. Baden-Powell raised an admonitory finger.

"What's the hurry? Have you forgotten Kim and his haste? Gabbling won't make you any more efficient, Jan. Only by doing something many times will it get done perfectly. That makes it worth doing." That reminded him of the evenings spent with Kipling at 'The Woolsack' before the war, correcting the proofs for 'Aids to Scouting', picking over every idea meticulously with another man who loved children and the outdoors. When Kipling had lived in Vermont he marveled at the turning of the leaves each autumn. Tragically his eldest daughter, Josephine, had died of pneumonia two years previously on a visit to America at the age of seven. His only son would die at eighteen on the Flemish front, encouraged by his patriotic father to enlist and fight for king and country.

Baden-Powell observed and deduced. For him a good scout possessed eyes in the back of his head. He noticed trifling details both near and at a distance, details that escaped the attention of ordinary people. Sometimes it backfired. His colleagues teased him about it. The Juta children enjoyed one tale particularly. The incident took place in the gardens of Ottershaw Park. Baden-Powell was walking with Violet, the young daughter of the Earl of Meath, when she suddenly pointed to footprints on the path and asked him what they meant.

"A common or garden cat has recently passed this way," he guessed confidently. Violet stamped her foot.

"Yes. Any child could tell you that, Colonel!" she complained. "I can further tell you the color of the cat. Can you?" Such a challenge immediately put Baden-Powell on his mettle. He set to work to examine any protruding twig or leaf that might have snared a hair from the passing animal. Search as he would, he found no clue that would indicate the color of the cat. Violet tossed her head.

"Well, if I am not mistaken," she said, looking more closely at the path, "it was a light tortoise-shell cat." Her companion also looked attentively at the ground, but could detect nothing helpful. He confessed himself beaten.

"How on earth did you arrive at the color?" he demanded. Violet shrugged her shoulders.

"I saw the cat," she said. The children giggled at the tale they had heard a dozen times and wondered what game Baden-Powell had in mind today. He put a hand into his capacious breast pocket and retrieved a fistful of colored cloth scraps and handed them to Luia.

"Jan and I will give you ten minutes and then we'll be on your trail. It better be a good one, eh, Jan?" Luia scampered off in the direction of Wynberg Hill as fast as her rather plump legs would carry her. She laid a trail of colored rags diligently and as diversely as possible. Sometimes she laid them on the ground, sometimes snared on bushes, sometimes hung in the fork of a tree. She had soon left the sandy rutted Herschel Walk well behind and turned south towards the shallow Liesbeek Valley. She enjoyed running by the river most, a special, almost sacred place. The quiet slow-moving stream meandered among pine and oak trees. The high slate roofs of Bishop's Court came and went beyond the swaying branches. In the vast grounds lay the ruins of a cottage, home to a local legend that still circulated among the older Cape families. A famous surgeon, Dr. James Barry had once occupied the cottage. He lived there peacefully with his daughter and a deaf-and-dumb colored servant, until the daughter of the Governor General fell in love with him. The doctor received the declaration unenthusiastically. This indifference provoked a duel with one of the lady's more passionate suitors and Dr. Barry received a serious wound. He was consequently discovered to be a woman, the mistress, in fact, of the Governor General! The Juta children often sat on the ruined foundation walls and dangled their feet in the clear rippling water.

Luia came to a halt. All round her the shadowy woods rang to the melodious chorus of lovebirds, babblers, slender-billed pipits and long-tailed yellow and green wagtails. Among the swaying arundo grasses and purple water irises, brilliant metallic blue dragonflies flitted and swooped, transparent-winged and wonderfully ephemeral. They fitted well with the romantic tale of the Governor's mysterious mistress. Luia sat on a fallen oak trunk, half submerged in the eddying water. A startled hare sprang wild-eyed from a nearby coppice and bounded into the underbrush. A carpenter bee alighted beside her on the trunk to investigate a strip of decaying bark. The powdery wood fanned out in a fine yellow spray under its wings. When Baden-Powell with Jan in tow appeared ten minutes later, Luia still sat silent by the stream, watching the wavering weeds in the current and the silver sheen of water washing over the magnified bed of pure white pebbles.

8

Luia Juta would always remember Rhodes as the man who told her about the eight birds, carved from soapstone, found in the ruins of Zimbabwe. The walls of the old capital, constructed without mortar, rose over twenty feet high. When Rhodes had first seen the mediaeval monument, he saw it as a sign of the great riches the area would yield. He hired the archeologist, Theodore Bent, to undertake excavations and publish the results. Bent, whose archeological experience had all been in Greece and Asia Minor believed the massive fortress to have been built by the Arabs. Later excavations would conclude that the site was of Bantu origin.

From her vantage point astride the stoep balustrade, Luia watched the governess' voluminous white hat floating above the hydrangeas as she strolled through the field to 'The Woolsack'. The honeysuckle and bougainvillea on the summerhouse trellis buzzed with bees. The soporific droning lulled her to drowsiness and she barely noticed the flock of black-bibbed house sparrows disputing with high-pitched chirps the remains of a water melon outside the kitchen door. Her somnolence was shattered by the shrill voice of a girl reciting aloud in the Kipling's garden.

"Out of this wood do not desire to go. Thou shalt remain here, whether thou wilt or no. I am a spirit of no common rate." Beyond the patchwork honeysuckle shade Luia recognized Elsie Kipling, holding a heavy leather-bound book at arm's length. She looked and sounded terribly serious. In her free hand she twirled a sprig of bright yellow sorrel. Every ten seconds she stopped talking to sniff the blossoms.

"Sorrel doesn't have any smell, you know," said Luia, poking her head through a gap in the fence. Elsie stopped pacing and contemplated the bunch of flowers. She thought for a second.

"I know it doesn't", she retorted impatiently. She threw the flowers away. They lay scattered and suddenly pointless on the trampled gravel. Luia ignored the rebuff.

"What are you reading?" she enquired, turning her head to try and decipher the gold letters on the spine. She had recognized the lines as Shakespearean, having had to learn them long ago for her father. She couldn't remember which play they came from.

"I'm learning them," replied Elsie evasively. The coolness of her reception was meant to convey the message that girls of twelve only deigned speak to girls of ten from common courtesy. "We're acting a play," she relented.

"Who's 'we'?" Luia wondered.

"Daddy and John and I, of course. I'm Titania." From her tone of voice, Luia couldn't decide whether her companion was proud or bored at the prospect. Luia loved the theatre. Her parents had recently taken her to see a play by Oscar Wilde, 'The Importance of being Ernest'. She would have liked to play the role of Lady Bracknell. "A handbag!" She had heard her parents talking afterwards about how Wilde had died in Paris two years ago after going to prison. She had asked why and her mother said it was for something not very nice and certainly not suitable for little girls' ears. Henry Juta, however, said that Wilde would be remembered as the greatest talker of his age, a genius and a man of wide learning and humanity.

Visibly Elsie Kipling had difficulty learning the lines and even understanding their meaning. The only fun to be had consisted in helping her father make Bottom's ass's head out of papier maché.

"I'll test you, if you like," proposed Luia a little patronizingly. Actually she felt a bit envious. She adored acting.

When he found the time, Henry Juta wrote small sketches for the children to be performed before the guests at 'Mon Desir'. Both she and Jan had passed through the initial induction stage, when their older sisters cast them as the dog. They were sat under a rug and had to bark when anyone kicked them! Two recent guests had begged Sir Henry to allow Luia to return to England with them and train for the stage. Gilbert Parker, the Canadian novelist and imperialist politician, knighted recently for his service to Canadian literature, had been enthusiastic about Luia's singing of the 'Indian Love Lyrics' by Amelia Woodforde-Finden. The composer had married a lieutenant colonel in the Bengal Cavalry and lived in India. The sentimental 'Kasmiri Song' had been an instant success and Luia sang it with such conviction that another guest offered to have Luia trained in London. Not surprisingly, these propositions met with a firm refusal from Henry Juta and all hope of becoming a reincarnated Sarah Siddons ended there for the moment.

Luia took the volume of Shakespeare from Elsie and looked for where Titania's speeches had been underlined.

"What comes after the fairies say 'Where shall we go?'" she asked. Elsie pretended to think. In fact she had caught sight of a dung beetle pushing a ball of earth through the grass. Where would fairies go anyway? Into cowslips and under toadstools? If they did, then they hid themselves pretty well. How many times, when she was a little girl, had she pulled all the petals off a flower to find the fairy!

"Why don't you ask Daddy to give you a part?" she said finally. "You can be Titania, if you like. I don't mind. I can be a fairy. I can play Cobweb." Luia pursed her lips. She didn't want to appear too desperate for a part. "Let's go and ask Daddy," Elsie cried, jumping at the unexpected chance of escape from the role of a woman who said incomprehensible things to a man wearing a donkey's head. Luia glanced across the park. Miss Palmer still floated, opaque and papillaceous, among the blue hydrangeas.

"All right," she agreed, "but I mustn't be too long. Miss Palmer..." She broke off, conscious of the distressing and undignified fact that being under the close supervision of a governess didn't fit at all her role as a superior and emancipated young lady about to play the part of a fairy queen. She followed Elsie through the eucalyptus trees in search of Rudyard Kipling. They found the writer finishing his siesta on the stoep of 'The Woolsack', a habit acquired in India, where few Europeans survived the humid heat of afternoon except stretched out in a hammock under a mosquito net. In the shadow of Table Mountain, the modest single-storied bungalow with its arcade of whitewashed pillars nestled in a copse of leathery-leafed oaks. From the simple but tidy garden, a vast panorama opened across the cape flats to the distant Drakenstein hills, shrouded in a pale purple haze. The Malay gardener busied himself cutting back the myrtle and plumbago hedge surrounding the property on two sides. To the north a profusion of oleander and fig trees, wild cannas, arum lilies and wood violets had invaded the garden. Here Kipling had chosen to spend each winter, a very different prospect from the dust and flies of his boyhood Lahore or the biting arctic winds of Vermont or even the damp rainy winters of Sussex, where he had finally bought his lovely historical home.

The afternoon ritual began. Firstly they had to search for an unsplit banana leaf. This mission always ended in failure, although John had once found a leaf that was technically unsplit, but so dog-eared as to be scornfully eliminated by the majority. The two girls ran onto the roofed terrace. Kipling laid aside the book Elsie had been reading to him before he nodded off, 'The Lays of Ancient Rome'. Elsie had irritated him by mispronouncing certain words. What he termed as massacring the English language could drive him into a rage.

"The man who wrote these lines," he insisted, "went to the trouble of finding the exact sound that fitted the message he was trying to communicate. The least you can do is not to deform it!" he grumbled. With a start he realized how long he had dozed. His typewriter waited in the poky room he used as a study. Beside it lay scattered a miscellaneous jumble of fragmentary ideas he had collected, mostly animal stories he had so often told his children as a joke, until a cousin suggested that other children, all children, might enjoy reading the stories. John and Elsie emerged from the pine wood to announce that they had finished building the new 'story-telling' house. It replaced the old sacred altar that a recent gale had demolished.

"Come and see the new shrine," they called from the garden. Kipling glanced at the pile of unfinished manuscripts and sighed. Then he remembered his dead daughter and how she had loved listening to his tales. It made them even more precious. He allowed himself to be led into the wood to inspect the new hut, little more than a shell of interlaced pine branches. Once inside and squatting on the carpet of needles like an Indian chief conducting a pow-wow, Kipling's face brightened and reflected a love and understanding of youth, so dominant in his character. His childlike imagination had already given the world boy heroes like Kim and Stalky and Mowgli. Others lingered unborn still behind his thick glasses. His inquisitive eyes registered all they lighted upon with a powerful and fruitful desire to 'find out'.

He noticed Luia wriggling restlessly in the sun-filtered shadows. In the last months she had become too chubby in the stomach and waist department to please her mother, who seemed to take it as a personal insult and had obliged her daughter to wear a close-fitting inflexible girdle to imprison the offending fat.

"What a sad little girl!" he exclaimed, filling his antiquated briar pipe. "Where's her smile gone today?" Luia ran a hand over her constricted abdomen.

"Mummy said I'm getting too fat," she explained ruefully. The truth, alas, could not be denied. What people condescendingly termed 'puppy fat' no longer had a place within the aristocratic walls of 'Mon Desir'. A plump little girl was one thing; an overweight young lady quite something else! Kipling thought for a moment. He began humming to himself. The children knew what that meant. Most of Kipling's verse began with a hymn tune. He took off his glasses and began wiping them meticulously.

"In the sea, once upon a time, O my best beloved, there was a whale and he ate fishes. He ate the starfish and the garfish, the crab and the drab, the plaice and the dace, the skate and his mate, the mackerel and the pickerel, and the really truly twirly-whirly eel. All the fishes he could find in all the sea he ate with his mouth - so!" Luia sat up.

"He can't have eaten all the fish, you know" she objected.

"Quite right, young lady. He did not eat all the fish. There was one small fish left in all the seas, and he was a small stutefish, and he swam a little behind the whale's right ear.

"Whales don't have ears," insisted Jan.

"This one did." Kipling opened the sketch pad he always carried with him and began drawing the strangest whale they had ever seen. "This whale belonged to a very rare species of eared whales, the 'balaena auricula' in Latin. Nice-looking fellow, isn't he? Anyway, the whale stood up on his tail. He could do that too," he added quickly before anyone had time to raise an objection. "He got that habit from a great-grandfather, Balaena Caudatus, who had died in the year 1777. As I was saying, the whale got up on his caudatus and said 'I'm hungry!' and the small stutefish said in a small stute voice:

"Noble and generous cetacean, have you ever tasted Man?"

"No" said the whale. "What's it like?"

"Nice," said the small stutefish. "Nice but nubbly."

"Then fetch me some," ordered the whale and he made the sea froth with his tail.

"One at a time is enough," said the stutefish. "If you swim to latitude 50° north, longitude 40° west you will find, sitting on a raft in the middle of the sea, with nothing on but a pair of blue canvas breeches and a pair of suspenders..." Kipling turned to Luia. "You must not forget the suspenders, best beloved," he said. Luia blushed and looked down to see if perhaps one of her blue stockings had come loose and slipped below her knee. Kipling winked and went on. "...you will find one shipwrecked mariner who, it is only fair to tell you, is a man in infinite resource and sagacity." None of the children knew what 'sagacity' meant, but they weren't going to interrupt a good story for such an insignificant detail. John had vague visions of sago puddings and the mariner eating them on his raft. Luia thought it might have something to do with the Sargasso Sea.

Kipling managed finally to light his refractory pipe and watched with pleasure the delicate plume of blue smoke rise serenely into the domed ceiling of pine branches. As always the smoke recalled memories: three years ago, lying delirious in a New York hotel bedroom, unaware of the hushed crowds outside on 7th Avenue, unaware of his dying daughter a few miles away; Lahore thirty-three years ago, a sunburnt sahib's son astride the canon on its brick platform outside the museum where his father worked; Vermont eleven years ago, 30° below zero, taking sleigh rides with Carrie, wrapped warmly in buffalo hides and goatskin caps; Westward Ho twenty years ago, sprawled on the summer cliffs among the clumps of yellow-bloomed gorse, with Lundy Island smudging the horizon and the channel tide hissing over the smooth sea-washed shingle a hundred feet below.

"Daddy! The story!" Elsie stamped her foot, too familiar with her father's tendency to drift off into the past, a friendlier world before Josephine's untimely death. "Did the whale find the mariner?"

"He did indeed, Elsie. Why?"

"And did he eat him?" John asked, still struggling with sago puddings. Kipling sucked voluptuously on his pipe.

"And ate him. He opened his mouth back and back and back till it nearly touched his tail and he swallowed the shipwrecked mariner and the raft he was sitting on and his blue canvas breeches and the girdle—I beg your pardon, Luia—and the suspenders, which you must not forget. He swallowed them all down into his warm dark inside cupboard.

Then he smacked his lips—so! and turned round three times on his tail."

In the ensuing silence, the children tried to imagine what a whale might look like on its tail, swallowing a shipwrecked mariner eating a sago pudding on a raft. With a chuckle, Kipling opened his sketchbook again. He uncorked a tiny bottle of Indian ink, brushed away the pine needles and began drawing. He had always loved sketching or better still drawing maps of imaginary places. One of his favorite pastimes was faking old documents. He would age them by carefully rubbing the paper with soot and dust. He often painted masks and crowns for children's fancy dress parties and made false noses to frighten old ladies. He finished his sketch.

"There now. Here we have the enterprising whale swallowing the mariner with his infinite resource and sagacity and his raft and his suspenders. Those buttony things here are the suspenders. He has a knife close by them. He is sitting on the raft, but it has tilted sideways, so you don't see much of it. The whitey thing by his left hand is a piece of wood that he was trying to row the raft with when the whale came along. That piece of wood is called the 'jaws of a gaff'. The mariner left it outside when he went in." The enthralled children peered over his shoulder, watching the picture take form before their eyes. In their secure cocoon of pine boughs they could hear the wind's muted moan overhead and the incessant cooing of doves. Flies buzzed in the resin-scented shadows. A carriage swung round the drive leading to Groote Schuur.

Kipling finished his drawing and recorked the ink bottle. "The whale's name was Smiler," he told them. "And the mariner was called Mr. Henry Albert Bivvens, A.B."

"Where's the stutefish?" asked John anxiously.

"The stutefish is hiding under the whale's tummy, which is why I haven't drawn him in," Kipling explained. "The reason that the sea looks so ooshy-skooshy is because the whale is sucking it all into his mouth, so as to suck in Mr. Henry Albert Bivvens and the raft and the suspenders."

The drawing took another ten minutes to complete and the story another fifteen. It appeared that the ingurgitated mariner kicked up such a fuss inside the whale with his hornpipes that the afflicted beast got the hiccoughs. In fact by the time the mariner had persuaded the whale to swim him back to England, he had cut up his raft to make a square grating tied together with his suspenders. He dragged this grating into the whale's throat and stepped out onto the shingle. Kipling peered over the thick black rims of the glasses.

"Which is why, my dears," he exclaimed, whales never swallow Men." The shadows on Table Mountain had lengthened noticeably. Long shafts of the setting sun sheared off the rose-tinted cliffs, clear and sharp on the heights, but diffused and opaque as the gloom of dusk descended on the vineyard terraces that climbed the lower slopes. Luia jumped to her feet. She had heard Miss Palmer's war cry from the top of the garden.

"You'd better answer the call, young lady." Kipling tore out the sketch and handed it to her. "Take this along as evidence," he proposed with another wink. With Jan in tow, Luia scampered up the steep woodland path towards home. She had forgotten Titania. She saw only the flapping white hat, sailing majestically on the far side of the banana hedge, silhouetted against the red rim of the sinking sun behind the crenellated summit ridges of Devil's Peak,

In the Muizenberg cottage Cecil Rhodes lay struggling for breath by a gaping hole in the seaward wall. He had ordered the wall to be knocked out in the hope of catching the cool ocean breezes. On the stoep a colored servant pumped a punkah through the other window with the faltering throb of a failing heart beat. On the dusty beachside lane a patient crowd had gathered outside the gate, perplexed pilgrims before a shrine, waiting for a slice of history to slip through their fingers, so that one day they could say they had been present when the great statesman died. From time to time Dr. Jameson or Philip Jourdain appeared at the door for a quiet chat and a cigarette.

Luia and Jan Juta had spent the afternoon among the low tide rocks. On the way home they noticed the crowd motionless and silent by the fence. They had been told that Mr. Rhodes was too unwell to invite them in for tea any more. There would be no more stories about the veldt and mysterious lands beyond the Limpopo River.

Prostrate on his bed, Rhodes hardly noticed the patient Jameson who never left his side, day or night, except for a short doze on the sofa. From time to time he muttered something and the doctor put his ear close to the dying man's mouth.

"You know, Jameson, the world today is nearly all parceled out, and what there is left of it, is being divided up, conquered and colonized. I would annex the planets if I could!" Eventually even his mind wavered, leaving little more than a vacuous smile on his blue lips. Only in the more lucid moments did he return to his plans for a scholarship program. "My students must not be merely bookworms. They shall have qualities of... you know what I mean, Jameson. Say it. Say it."

"They must be men."

"Yes. Manhood, truth, courage, devotion to duty, sympathy for and protection of the weak, kindliness, unselfishness and fellowship. Men who aren't afraid to act for fear of making a mistake," he added, repeating Baden-Powell's favorite maxim. Only the wheeze of the punkah and the subdued murmur of the crowd in the lane broke the despondent silence. Rhodes' disorganized thoughts roamed over the pages of dictated notes abandoned in his study at Groote Schuur. The chilling present had faded into the warm security of the past: all those blazing sunsets over Hanghoek farmsteads, over fields of proteas at Somerset West, strings of herring gulls on the fishing harbor at Hermanus, on the bright red and purple springtime flats at Worcester, all the South African veldt with its gently undulating slopes of golden daisies and the grass below, dry and brittle and burning.

Finally he dozed off, stretched on his back with open mouth. Jameson got quietly to his feet and left the room. He had taken no rest for three days. His head ached. His arms and legs had lost all sensation. Only Grimmer remained like a faithful dog to watch over his master. In his low gruff voice he talked to the dying politician of the old days on the veldt. He administered his medicine. Once or twice the dying flame flared up and Rhodes mustered the strength to rebuff the proffered help.

"I see no reason why I should make my interior a dustbin for anyone!" he grumbled between gulps. Grimmer cajoled and crooned like an old nanny about to burst into tears.

The end came mercifully soon. From the stoep Jameson heard Rhodes calling him in a loud clear voice. Half an hour later, when the first close friends began to arrive, they found the doctor in tears, alone at the window, fumbling with the curtains, with his back to the dead man on the bed.

Three days later the night train from Cape Town puffed laboriously up the steep gradient over Sir Lowry's Pass in the Hottentot Mountains. The folded strata of orange rock reflected the sunset with the burnish of beaten copper. Passengers admiring the view through the pass to the Cape coast far below had to shield their eyes. Wisps of drifting cloud lingered over the surrounding summits. Henry Juta returned to the paper he had been reading. Unconsciously his mind had registered the passing landscape, apparently so barren, but teeming with an amazing variety of floral life: red Afrikaner, prickly clumps of steekbossie, geelbos and scarlet klokkieshei. He thought of Jan Smuts and his love of botany. His colleague from the Cape Town bar had become a guerilla fighter, leading commandoes deep into British territory to foment rebellion. He would, however, soon conclude realistically that it were wiser to come to terms and negotiate a peace treaty.

At the front of the train lay Rhodes' elaborate coffin, made of costly Matabele teak. As a past Speaker of the Cape House of Assembly and legal advisor to the dead Prime Minister, Sir Henry had been invited to attend the funeral ceremonies to be held among the Matopo Hills near

Bulawayo in the heart of Rhodesia. Despite serious opposition from his wife, Henry Juta had decided to take Luia on
the trip. Already over-excited at the prospect of her immi-
nent departure for school in England, in the footsteps of her
three sisters, it would be the only occasion Luia might ever
have of visiting the country of her birth before she left it for
good. Absurdly he remembered an incident that epitomized
his relationship with the youngest of his daughters. On the
day of his inauguration as Speaker of the House, splendidly
attired in his robes, he had appeared with his family at the
top of the flight of stairs leading to the hall. He noticed
Luia fidgeting beside him and to his horror saw her flannel
petticoat slipping slowly down her legs. Before he had time
to react, Helen Juta whispered: "Pick it up, darling, like a
handkerchief, and give it to me."

Juta took out his watch. It would soon be time to go along
to the dining-car. In the next compartment Rudyard Kipling
opened the evening paper. The latest news indicated that the
end of the war was only a matter of days away. Nevertheless,
lieutenant-general Methuen had not only suffered defeat at
Magersfontein, but had been captured, the only British general to be made prisoner during the war. He had been wounded
in the battle as well as breaking his leg after his horse fell on
him. The Boer general Koos de la Rey had released him,
due to the severity of his injuries and even provided his personal cart to take Methuen to hospital in Klerksdorp. Kipling
thumped the paper indignantly.

"We've had a jolly good lesson, and it serves us jolly well
right!" Henry Juta smiled wistfully.

"I wonder why it is that people can never learn the value
of compromise," he remarked. Kipling snorted.

"Compromise be blowed! Never forget that the outward
and visible signs of our authority must always prevail before
a native."

"I hadn't really thought of the Dutch as natives," objected
Juta with raised eyebrows. No wonder people attacked
Kipling for his imperialist politics. He had once stated to

the press that only the 'lesser breeds' were born beyond the English Channel.

The distant ringing of the dinner bell woke Luia. Outside the compartment window night had fallen. Here and there a solitary amber lamp signaled an isolated farmstead in the immensity of the nocturnal veldt. Her book lay open on the floor and she stooped to pick it up. The excitement of this second state ceremony she had attended with her father returned. The other occasion had been an official lunch with a Zulu chief, when she had eaten grilled caterpillars on sticks without knowing what they were. This would be her first funeral. Of course, when Queen Victoria had died a few months ago, the whole house had gone into mourning, but that wasn't a real funeral with a coffin and flowers.

Luia clung to her father's arm as they lurched down the swaying carriage to the dining-car. Henry Juta knew most of the other diners, friends of Rhodes or prominent political figures. At least they had been spared the presence of Catherine Radziwill. Securely locked up in Roeland Street jail, the princess awaited a third trial on twenty-four counts of fraud and forgery. Many people went so far as to blame her for Rhodes' premature death. She had sullied his good name without a shadow of justification and he never lived to see his name completely cleared.

"Five days I think Grimmer said, didn't he?" asked Kipling about the length of the train journey to Bulawayo.

"At least five days," Juta replied. "We shall have to bypass Vryburg." The small agricultural town had housed a notorious concentration camp for Boer women and children until it fell into enemy hands. To complicate the long journey, the train stopped continually at wayside stations wreathed in flowers. At the lamp-lit dinner tables discussions turned round the projected funeral plans. At Bulawayo the coffin would be loaded onto an ox cart and transported twenty miles south into the hills to be buried on the site Rhodes himself had chosen on the summit of Malindidzimu, the 'hill of spirits'. The hills had been formed over two thousand million years ago with granite being forced to the surface and then eroded to produce smooth whaleback 'dwalas' and broken kopjes, strewn with boulders and interspersed with thickets of vegetation. Perhaps one or two people might even remember that Malindidzimu was also the site of the Matabele stronghold into which Rhodes had walked, alone and unarmed, to negotiate peace with chief Ndebele.

Kipling had been asked to read a valedictory poem of his own composition. He had begun it while the body lay in state in Cape Town cathedral. Now he drank his soup and listened to the metronomic clicking of the wheels over the rails and let the words revolve to the rhythm of the moving train.

"The immense and brooding Spirit still shall quicken and control. Living he was the land, and dead his soul shall be her soul."

Epilogue

On April 17th, 1904 the royal mail ship 'Saxon' weighed anchor and slid silently away from the quay. A small crowd stood waving in front of the customs building. A few had walked to the end of the mole, where a knot of boys sat fishing among the screaming seagulls. Luia Juta stood on the first class deck between her father and Thomas Brassey, the governor of Victoria on his way home from Australia. Brassey had been the first man to circumnavigate the globe in his schooner 'Sunbeam'

Like a well-oiled piece of machinery things that had to be had come to pass. Her three sisters had left South Africa and now it was Luia's turn. She stood at the rail and watched Table Mountain sinking into the sea and tried to put into words those twelve years in a fairy story world that now existed only in the past. She would have to preserve a South Africa above all other South Africas that might sneak into her memory in the years to come: those long evenings on the veldt with her father and Cecil Rhodes during a shooting trip; nights under the Karroo sky, the immense sapphire catafalque, studded with myriads of stars.

"My idea is to create equal rights for every civilized man south of the Zambesi," the millionaire is saying. In reply a lion roars in the pitch-black bush. "What is a civilized man? A man whether white or black who has sufficient education to write his name and is not a loafer. I don't care about those who lie on their backs in the sun all day." The smoke from the men's pipes curls up into the overhanging branches of the baobab. The lion coughs again a little nearer and the haunting sound rolls round the sleeping hills. Then slowly, very slowly, it fades into the timeless mystery of memory.